ALSO BY BETH KEPHART

A Slant of Sun: One Child's Courage

Into the Tangle of Friendship:
A Memoir of the Things That Matter

STILL LOVE
IN STRANGE
PLACES

~~~

A Memoir

BETH KEPHART

W. W. NORTON & COMPANY
NEW YORK   LONDON

972.8405
K38

The text of this book is composed in Bembo with the display set in Bembo
Composition by Roy Tedoff
Manufacturing by Quebecor World, Fairfield
Book design by Mary A. Wirth
Production manager: Amanda Morrison

Library of Congress Cataloging-in-Publication Data
Kephart, Beth.
Still love in strange places : a memoir / Beth Kephart
p. cm.
ISBN 0-393-05074-2
1. El Salvador—Description and travel. 2. Kephart, Beth. I. Title.

F1484.3 .K47 2002
972.8405'3—dc21   2001055770

W. W. Norton & Company, Inc., 500 Fifth Avenue, New York, N.Y. 10110
www.wwnorton.com

W. W. Norton & Company Ltd., Castle House, 75/76 Wells Street,
London W1T 3QT

1 2 3 4 5 6 7 8 9 0

For Bill
where the story begins

And for Jeremy
where it begins again

———∞∞∞———

CONTENTS

Old shoes, St. Anthony's Farm

PROLOGUE

---

*S*till *Love in Strange Places* is about romance and land,
memory and imagination, exile and acceptance. Its setting is El Salvador, my husband's home. Its protagonist
is a coffee farm high in the jungle hills. Its purpose is to
explore the ways we arrive at what we love, the ways we
surrender what we fear, the ways stories rescue us from
the strangeness of each other.

El Salvador has had a hold on my imagination since
I met my husband more than eighteen years ago. I have
been afraid, uneasy, resentful, distrustful, and always, at
the same time, beguiled and impassioned. I have been
drawn in by the facts of the land itself—by how the
Central American land bridge essentially rose from the
seas late in the history of our planet, creating a byway of
exchange and opportunity between two previously
independent continents. I have found myself mired in
native myths about mischievous dogs and deviant
witches, about oxcarts that rattle toward the dying at
night. I have fallen in love with the tales of Carlos
Alberto Bondanza, my husband's grandfather, who
escaped his own execution, survived the bloody
matanza, and tended St. Anthony's Farm in amicable

cooperation with the campesinos, even as more rumors of class revolution and war rumbled across his country.

Finally, I have come to respect the way my sixty-eight-year-old mother-in-law today upholds the traditions of St. Anthony's—her country left ragged after many years of civil war, her husband gone, her sons departed, her one leg long ago gone limp. With overarching decency and a pragmatic sense of humor, with an awkward leg brace and a guard at her back, she today rules the land her father left her with an even disposition, delivering secondhand shoes to the peasants in their cardboard huts, buying teeth for the toothless, hauling used clothes up from the city, and demanding, all the while, a clear and careful and honest picking of her coffee when it ripens in December. This she does without having any certain answer as to who will love the land when she is gone.

Coffee is not native to El Salvador; it was first commercially planted there in 1839 by a Brazilian pedagogue named Antonio J. Coelho. And yet, today, El Salvador is, in many ways, defined by its coffee—by the annual yields, by the organization of the farms, by the peace that is or is not kept by those who work the trees in those volcanic jungles. Everywhere one looks, pressures—on natural resources, on money, on patience, on faith—abound. Still, the traditions at St. Anthony's continue.

When I married my husband, I married into all of this. I married a legacy, traditions, danger. I married a man who is not at home unless he's standing in the shadows of his grandfather's land or asserting the privileges of a jeep on jungle roads. My husband isn't home here, where we together live, and yet years would go by before I could begin to understand, before my imagination would let me close to where he'd come from. In moving closer to him, I forfeited parts of myself. I asserted myself in a place where I—a conservative, American, risk-averse woman—hardly thought I would ever belong.

— *JUNE 2001*

The road above El Limón

In the soils of El Salvador, anything can grow. Flick the pit of a mango to the ground, and tomorrow there'll be a tree. Tell a story, and the story grows, its roots tapping down into one's dreams.

STILL LOVE
IN STRANGE
PLACES

Carlos Alberto Bondanza (*right*), with gratitude to
Adela for sharing the photograph

TORN PHOTOGRAPH,
SEPIA STAINED

—⌘—

*T*he tear runs like a river through a map, hurtling down toward his right shoulder, veering threateningly at his neck, then diverting south only to again pivot east at the fifth brass button of his captain's uniform. Below the tear, two more brass buttons and the clasp of his hands and, below all that, the military saber; the loosening creases on his pants; the shoes with their reflections of the snap of camera light. He is one of three in a sepia-colored portrait, and someone had to think to save his face. Someone had to put the photo back together—re-adhere the northeast quadrant of this map with three trapezoids of tape so that his left hand would fall again from his left elbow and he would still belong to us. We suppose he is the best man at a wedding. We suppose that it was eighty years ago, before the *matanza*, before he was jailed and then set free, before he saved the money to buy the land that became St. Anthony's Farm.

"Did I ever tell you what my grandfather did the year the farm first turned a profit?"

"No."

"He threw the money into the air, the bills, and they got caught up with a wind."

"And so?"

"And so he ran after those colones through the park. Chased his own money through the leafy streets of Santa Tecla. Imagine that."

I do. I am often imagining that. Imagining that I know him—this man whose likeness is my husband's face, whose features are now borne out by my son. His are the sepia eyes that passed through me. His is the broad nose, the high cheekbones, the determined mouth, the face not like an oval or a heart, but like a square. He died long before I'd ever meet him, but I carried him in my blood. Just as the land carries him still, remembers. Just as St. Anthony's Farm will someday, in part, belong to my son, requiring him to remember what he never really knew, to put a story with the past. Words are the weights that hold our histories in place. They are the stones that a family passes on, hand to hand, if the hands are open, if the hearts are.

"You look like your great-grandfather."

"I do?"

"Yes. Come here. See? That's him, in the photograph."

"Him? My great-grandfather?"

"Yes."

"But he looks so young."

"Well, he was young once. But that was a long time ago, in El Salvador."

We remember. We imagine. We pass it down. We step across and through a marriage, retrieve the legacies for a son.

St. Anthony's Farm rises above a town called El Limón, above a river you can hear but cannot see. It rises at an angle that would pitch any mortal down, were it not for the trees, standing so densely close, each limb like a hand to hold, a brace. The trees that yield the *Coffea arabica* need height and cool to grow.

Sun for only hours at a time. Soil rich in potash, nitrogen, phosphoric acid; preferably disintegrated volcanic rock.

It's after the monsoon rains in May that white blossoms erupt from these stalwart trees—star-shaped, exuberant flowers that fill the air with a honeysuckle sweetness. And it's after the flowers dissipate that you find the nubs of cherries—emerald green at first, knuckled about the branches like so many determined fists as they slowly fatten, brighten with the sun. By December the fruit is ready and the pickers have come, taken up their places in the constricted alleys between the trees. You see their head scarves among the leaves—bright yellow, orange, green. You see the plastic bags of purple juice and the stack of cold tortillas that wait beside their feet, beside their baskets and their burlap bags, worn burlap bags, noticeably mended. You see their children gambol down the narrow, beveled paths, their own baskets hanging from a length of rope or a strap of worn leather about their necks, their smiles like sudden crescent moons amid the shadows. Hummingbirds rustle in the shade trees overhead. Beetles bicker. Dragonflies buzz in and out of the shrapnel flecks of light.

I married all this when I married my husband. I married a foreign language and a national preoccupation with a witch named Siguanaba and butterflies large as kittens. El Salvador, the Savior. The size of Massachusetts. The politics of oppression. The peril of a swatch of earth that trembles still above its fault lines. *When I was a kid . . . ,* I've heard my husband say on the path ahead. *Before the war . . . . When my grandfather was alive . . . .* The past in the present. A man long gone who is still, by a kind of miracle, alive.

Carlos Alberto Bondanza was Bill's grandfather's name. He remains a legend among those who yearly come to free the coffee cherries from the trees. They remember the priest he'd bring to the hills. The fruit trees he invented. The parcels of land he rented for free to those he trusted with his coffee. They remember the silence he brought on with his siesta, and the hen-like *chacha* that he coaxed into mating with the pheasant, playing like God in the hills. His feat, they say, was living well. His feat was not living at the expense of others.

*H*e died of cancer, and Bill's lasting regret is that he did not die among the coffee trees. "I should have kidnapped him from that sick room and taken him up the road to the hills. But you know how that road is," he now says, and I do; this part I understand.

Today the trip from the city house in Santa Tecla to the farm above El Limón is its own indigenous form of torture—not just the traffic but all that's inclined toward erosion. To get above the city, one must first go straight through it, into and out of the mess of the marketplace. It's everything you imagine a city ringed by mountains is. The narrowed-to-nothing Pan-American Highway jammed with thin tin cars and huffy tractor-trailers and psychedelic buses that wear passengers on their roofs and on their running boards, on hemp ladders tied to the back where the exhaust pipes spew rubble with their smoke. The only relief is the park—one high-curbed, block-sized square of beaten grass, a few shade trees, a scattering of towering palms. There stands a makeshift wooden stage, where sometimes the mayor will preach or a marimba band will play or, in Decembers past, they would hold a beauty pageant for the Santa Tecla girls, allowing anyone who could afford to vote to buy their vote and crowning, consistently, the ugliest girl in town. It is in this park that Don Alberto once tossed his money to the sky. It is across its bordering tumultuous roadway where he maintained his city residence—a grand stucco edifice with a lush fruit-tree garden that I saw but once from a distance, some thirteen years ago, before bulldozers knocked it to the ground.

The marketplace is what the people have made it. It is the shabby, precarious architecture of hot metal lean-tos and cardboard roofs and blankets and milk crates and goods. Time and again the bureaucrats have tried to contain it, building block-long warehouses into which to stuff the merchants. Always the commerce has spilled back onto the streets, everything defiantly elbow to elbow. The charred pig on a stick beside the splitting sacks of coffee, the stalks of flowers keeping company with the fish, the shopkeepers fast asleep in their folding chairs, live chickens peeking out from haphazard shadows, and, of course: the corn-husk dolls, the rush-woven mats, the palm-leaf hats, the decorated gourds, the goose-feather powder puffs, the lidded baskets and the baskets made of vine. Coatepeque crabs have been known to get loose from merchant baskets and to scramble in among the hairy husks of corn or the hard white crusts of cheese, and all day long, on blackened dirty grills, on *comales*, with the help of smoothened *metates*, little girls make *pupusas* and tortillas. At one point the market depletes itself, and there are no stalls at all, nothing propped up overhead to ward off the relentless sun. Then there is only the sprawl of blankets, torn paper bags, faded newsprint that separates the women and the children from the direct heat of the earth. They come from miles away to sell whatever they have. They sit and they sleep in the streets.

You can see all that from your car or your jeep, as you sit in the stranglehold of traffic, the air so dense with gasoline that you finally swallow it down. You can hear its history in the tales that Bill will tell about the house where he was born—just over there, a barbershop now where his mother's sitting room once was—or about that bit of open space, now wreckage, where he would come and spin tops with his friends. You can hear the resonance in the stories he doesn't tell, in the secrets you know he's keeping, in the Spanish he preserves for himself, and you can be made to feel lonely, or you can be made to feel alive, alert, privileged, even, to be here beside him, to take this journey which is his, to be forced up against a place you'd hardly know of otherwise. You are forced, in El Salvador, to make decisions.

It can take five minutes or more to advance a single Santa Tecla block, and then another five minutes and you break free, turning left off the Pan-American Highway, then right and left again, snaking through the streets between hovels and merchants and pedestrians and drunks, the leathery old men pissing their *guaro* onto the many-fissured sidewalks. Today it's Bill's mother, Nora, at the wheel of our jeep, and nothing cows her; she fights the traffic and the serpent streets with everybody else until the asphalt turns to dirt and we hit the base of the coffee mountain, where it is poverty again, just a different color. But back then it would have been Bill at the wheel, his grandfather in the throes of the cancer beside him.

There would have been no way—no possible way—for Bill's grandfather to take this journey one last time. And still Bill dreams of what might have been. He dreams of settling a mat outside amid the aroma of the trees and giving Don Alberto a view of the land that became his. Giving him more time among the peasants who were the keepers of his farm, his friends. Giving him more time with Bill, who struggles to remember what he can in fact remember, to hold on to it and to give particles away, so that it can become somebody else's. His wife's: received, assimilated, and sometimes stolen. And, of course, his son's.

Coffee trees in January

BEGINNINGS

⸺⸺∞⸺⸺

*I*n the hooting, crawling, philandering shade of an over-grown jungle, high, near the sky, it is possible to imagine that the world is as the world always was. This is illusion, the chicanery of nature. For when it comes to Central America, to El Salvador, to St. Anthony's Farm, there was indeed a time, as the Maya say, when the sky seemed crashed against the earth, when there was darkness only, nothing at all. The land that forms Central America is erupted earth, the aftereffect of spectacular geological discontent, a land bridge suffering the wind and weather of two barely separated seas. Sixty million years ago, there was only ocean where the land bridge lies today. Eleven million years ago, there was but a single archipelago. Having risen from the volcanic sea in fits of calm and violence, that archipelago would be joined, over the course of many more millions of years, by additional by-products of glaciation and geological turbulence until the isthmian sill grew deeper and more and more land poked its nose up to the sky. The islands wouldn't connect, the pocked, swamped, peaking, dipping, hissing isthmian barrier wouldn't be complete, until three million years ago. But the cross-pollination of North and South American life was already in the works, so Central America was from the first an incubator of the exotic and inexplicable.

If we tend to forget that our lives are spent on the surface of things, it is nonetheless true: earthquakes, mountains, sea trenches, volcanoes, the continents themselves are ruled by matters far closer to our planet's core. The earth's rigid outer layer—thin where it is ocean floor, thicker where it is land—is in fact a series of plates. This lithosphere does not, most scientists suspect, control its own fate; instead, it is maneuvered by the mantle underneath. Since the mantle is closer to the molten iron center of the earth, it is also more volatile, more influential, propelling hot liquid rock all the way to the earth's surface in places, cooling and sinking elsewhere. It is this faithful turmoil that, it seems, dictates the movement of the lithospheric plates, and it is the collision, separation, aeration, and fracturing of the plates that explains, at least according to the plate-tectonic model, the mechanics of our shape-shifting planet, the birth of Central America, the emergence of tiny El Salvador.

The Maya, whose civilizations flourished from 1800 B.C. through A.D. 900 in the Yucatán, Guatemala, Chiapas, and parts of El Salvador, had their own ideas about where the land had come from, to what and whom the people owed their debt. In the Maya mind the universe passes through a series of endless cycles; our own universe, created on the thirteenth of August, 3114 B.C., is destined to fall on the twenty-third of December, A.D. 2012. An Armageddon preceded the current era—a great flood, the tumbling of sky into earth, the sudden snuffing out of light—and from the brew of nothingness arose a time of magic and godly stunts and two infamous pairs of twin brothers. The first set was punished for indulging in a raucous game of ball on the surface of the earth, then sacrificed. The second became famous for ridding the universe of an overbearing macaw, for sundry feats of trickery, for being killed and revived and finally being taken up to heaven as the sun and the moon.

And beneath the sun and moon was our own four-cornered earth, where every cardinal point was tinged with color: red for east, white for north, black for west, yellow for south. In the center of the universe stood a mighty blue-green tree—its branches spiking up to heaven, its roots thrusting down to the underworld, its presence a certain connection between the humans and the gods. Sometimes, in the eyes of the Maya, the earth was a crocodile floating in a bed of water lilies. Sometimes it was a turtle. Sometimes it was a cornfield or a house. And always the sun god rose from the east and began its travels across the sky. When it set in the west, it morphed into a jaguar, slipped down through the underworld, and clawed its way back east so as to be reborn at dawn as the sun.

It was an infested place: chiggers, horse spiders, black flies, juicy ants a full inch long. It was primordial and dangerously plagued with bats—nectar-drinking, insect-eating, papaya-favoring bats, as well as those that drink the blood of deer and cows, and those that sip at each other. And where the bats flew so did the butterflies, their wings transparent or midnight blue or masquerading as the disembodied eyes of owls, and where bats and butterflies flew, so flew the macaws—four or five dozen of them at once, scarlet, blue, gold, boastful, their hooked beaks capable of sinister songs. There was poison in that place—the green palm viper, the scorpion, the Hura tree with its blindness-inducing sap—and there were trees whose leaves, bark, and roots were full of persuasions against abscesses, infections, sores, fevers, toothaches, insects, and, inevitably, sadness, and whose branches bore the cloven sculpture of aerializing plants, philodendrons majestically spiraling from limb to lower limb.

Off on his own, hundreds of years later, Don Alberto could poke his stick in the ground to detect an underground spring. He could move his hands across the soil and calculate its potential generosity, its relative compatibility with coffee, fruit, or structure. He could watch the sun drizzle through the leaves and the ants come out when the heat had struck, and the wild flocks of vibrant parakeets bounce like atoms between the trees. Below him was the gorge, he could hear the river traveling, and on the other side of the mountain, the sounds of yet another farm, stray dogs, hungry chickens, dissatisfied pigs, timber being thrown onto a fire. Did this seem like forever to him? Did he think he could trust it? Sometimes, Bill says, he'd walk back up from the river with his Panama hat high on his head, calling his grandchildren from their distant playing places. When they had gathered around and he'd told some kind of story, he'd remove his hat and unveil a praying mantis sitting there. Ten inches long, at least, and brown, staring down from its perch on that white head.

The beauty, the danger, the impetuosity of the land is never backdrop in El Salvador; it is character, it is story, the place where things begin. This is what it took me years to learn, what I'm teaching now, to my son. I want him to imagine some two million years ago, when the land, new even to itself, played host to a caravan of creatures. Guided by intuition, hunger, boredom, curiosity, whatever it was that compelled them, the creatures set off across the land bridge on their own wild expeditions, the ones that could swim between the inchoate landmasses braving the virgin territory first, the nonswimmers forced to wait until the entire isthmus was emplaced. Up from South America came the bizarre, armor-toting glyptodonts, the small-, medium-, large-sized, and three-toed sloths, the swimming rats and spiny rats, the marmosets and porcupines, anteaters, opossums, armadillos, a gigantic, frightful bird, some nine feet tall, the *Titanis walleri*. From the north, the byways were crowded with shrews, with pocket mice and gophers, squirrels, big, beautiful cats, foxes, mastodons, horses, llamas, deer, raccoons. Persistent, wide-ranging, at risk, the species scurried their way in both directions across new earth, chomping at the flora as they migrated, trampling the grasses, the sensual orchids at their feet, feasting on one another or choosing to get along and produce their own odd animal young. They were farmers of a sort, change agents, thinning out rain forests, widening savanna swaths, swallowing seeds in the south and defecating them farther north, or doing it the other way around, so trees and flowers got put outside the zone of their natural occurrence, and birds and butterflies, in a whirl of colorful wings, migrated to their respective nectars. For hundreds of thousands of years, Central America and its species reinvented themselves without the interceding hand of man.

No one knows for certain when humans first arrived, though the mass extinction of literally dozens of large mammals—mastodons, mammoths, camels, ground sloths—something like eleven thousand years ago suggests to many that man had, by then, made his appearance. In any case, the human story in Central America has a hazy beginning, obfuscated by unproven possibilities and theories, by the absence of absolutism in fossils. Some paleontologists imagine early human hunting bands departing from Asia and trekking across the Bering land bridge, which had risen from the seas like some kind of braille during that ice cap era. They see the hunters moving south through a supposed interregnum in the ice cap, murdering the woolly mammoths and the mastodons as they went, converting the huge slain beasts into food, fuel, tools, and shelter and continually moving on, south, toward Arizona, Mexico, toward the land that would someday be christened Cuzcatlán. Others argue that the first Central Americans, hence El Salvadorans, came not via land but via sea, navigating their ingenious watercraft along the coast of Asia, or across the Atlantic waters, or coming by way not of North America but of South America, having forged the Pacific waters from their outposts in Australia, made it to land, and set off, north, on foot. Some date man's arrival there to twenty thousand years ago; others set the date closer to the extinction of large, strange mammals.

However it happened, from wherever they came, the early Indians of virgin El Salvador took immediate advantage of the volcano-dominated land, the land still jostled and woozy above the conspiratorial lithospheric plates. They lived a nomad's life: inhabiting caves and rock shelters, hunting fish and game, experimenting with the profoundly exotic flora, weaving vines into protective garments to ward off the pernicious insects, moving on when resources grew scarce. Such itinerancy ended with the domestication of maize, when the growing bands of Maya discovered how burning trees to the ground enriched the soil, how sticks poked into the darkened earth could make accommodating sleeves for the seeds. Maize was a stabilizer. The Maya civilization grew. Increasingly the soil was worked to depletion, until the earth became a quilt of yield and depletion, fallow stretches and plots that bloomed with maize, beans, squash, pumpkins, chile peppers.

The land was the mystery from which the Indians had come, the raw material upon which they staked their survival, the spirit and stuff to which they understood they would return, and for hundreds of years the Maya prospered. After A.D. 250 especially, hieroglyphic writing, books, calendars, star knowledge, human sacrifice, religion, even the mythological game with a rubber ball flourished as the Maya spread their civilization across the upper reaches of the isthmus. Society was further stratified. Rival city-states went to war. Land was at a perpetual premium—claimed and lost and claimed, burnt down, seeded, prayed over, used up, abandoned. It was plundered and bloodied, carved into temples, depleted. The Maya quarried the limestone and built. They carried rocks off the volcanic highlands and installed them in their kitchens to grind their maize. They turned obsidian into knives, lances, blades. They mined the salt. They plucked feathers and shells from the birds and the shore and glorified their kings. They extracted gold and jade from the streambeds of the imposing mountains, fired volcanic tuff into pots and colored those pots red with the paints they churned up with hematite iron ore. They boiled white lime in with the hard, ripe maize to bolster their diets with amino acids and niacin, understanding, somehow, that they would have died otherwise, that the kernels in their native form were not enough. Endowed with the luxuries of the land by their gods, the Maya put the land to work, and the land at last gave way. By A.D. 900, across Central America, the lowland riverside urban centers were abandoned for scattered, unstable cities in the hills. The classic age of the Maya had arrived, abruptly, at its end.

What caused the collapse remains just one more mystery. There are, as there always will be, theories. A widespread epidemic. A revolution of the Indian slaves against their ruthless masters. Troubles with trade or troubles with foreigners, too many internecine wars, the earth's own final hegemony: earthquake, drought. What is known is that things went bad in El Salvador, the Maya dissipated, and a new wave of settlers traipsed in to newly claim the land. The Pokomam Indians, settling in the west. The trade-minded Kekchi Indians of Guatemala. The Lenca Indians of Guatemala and Honduras. The Nahuatl Indians, who, in the eleventh century, migrated south from

Mexico with Aztec ways and founded the powerful kingdom of Cuzcatlán, a word, variously translated, that means happiness, richness, precious lands.

It was the Nahuatl who left their things behind in the land Don Alberto owned. He'd find their artifacts when he was digging out depleted trees, or when the campesinos cleared the land at the top of the farm where he built his house. Shards of fired pottery and broken deities, the clay porous but holding on, the implications overwhelming and finally, always, a mystery. The Nahuatl were farmers of maize, beans, tobacco, cocoa, pumpkins, gourds, seekers of long, flat, accommodating stretches of earth where their community-owned plots could thrive. There was always the question, for Don Alberto, for Bill, about why the Nahuatl had come to those hills, how long they'd stayed, how many there were, what they'd found, how they'd subsisted. Had they fought for the land with the last of the Maya, or had they found it empty? Was it an act of refuge or a simple accident? Had they settled or moved on? And what was it like to live on the land before it had known the cultivating forces of human hands, before even the Nahuatl or the Maya had made it home?

Salted fish for sale in La Libertad

SURVIVAL

I get the stories of Bill's grandfather from a man who, on principle, does not embellish. When I ask questions, Bill shrugs and says, *That part he didn't tell me.* When I need to see it and ask for proof, Bill says he can't help; I'll have to imagine. This has two effects: it narrows truth down; it opens truth up.

For example. Any number of times, according to Bill, Don Alberto should have died before he married the wife who would give him the daughter who would give birth to the man who became my husband, our only child's father. Once this death should have struck when Don Alberto, then close to thirty, a risk-taking swimmer, was trapped in the sucking fist of a Pacific whirlpool, far, far out, where he seemed destined to drown, but did not. Once when a shard of rock from a distant dynamite blast fatally pierced the skull of the man whom Don Alberto was sitting beside, sitting *immediately* next to, the two of them—one alive, one suddenly dead—astride their horses. Once he should have died during an incident that involved a cave that proved to be a tomb. The way Bill tells it, Don Alberto was in the jungle with yet another friend when a magnificent monsoon broke out and the two men, fearing for their lives, took refuge in a womb of carved-out rock. They were exhausted, it was dark, they were wet, they fell asleep. When dawn woke them with its jonquil light, when the fresh air cleared their nostrils and they could smell, they found a stranger newly dead (they presumed) from the disease raging then, tuberculosis—a corpse beneath a thicket of flies. The two friends stopped for nothing, Bill says, in their mad dash for the river. They tore lemons off of lemon trees and scoured their skin with yellow acids, to prevent infection.

"Tell me a story," I'll say to Bill, when it's late at night, too late, an irresponsible hour. If we could see outside, we'd see the naked spray of stars, the bony limbs of defiant trees, the pummeled yard with its white shocks of grass where our son plays soccer, digs for rabbits, tests the clayey, stingy soil. But the blinds are down and night comes to us in stealthy weightless flares.

"A story?"

"Another story."

"Well," he says. "Well." Choosing one he might have told before, or one that he's kept secret. "My grandfather," he'll say, after he's decided on that fragment of time that fits his mood, "was just a boy when he saw his father's uncle shot by the assassination squad of President Regalado." He'll pause, then he'll go on. "He hid behind the executioner's wall, and he could do nothing, he told me, to stop the murder, only scheme to rescue the dead man's bloody shirt. But I don't know whether he ever got the shirt, I can't remember, just now, how it went. Wait. Let me think . . . ."

It's late. Bill's voice drifts quietly toward me. Sometimes I fall asleep before I know how the story ends, before I'm sure, or Bill is, whether the blood-soaked shirt was retrieved. I wake a while afterwards, Bill himself asleep now in my arms. I wake ashamed that I did not hold out until the story's end.

This is how a person hears: with ears that grew out of gills. With the help of the delicate ossicles and the long tunnel of the eustachian tube, and the cochlea, which might itself have been found on a beach, among so many pristine shells. Sound is channeled in to a liquid place, then intercepted, converted, helped along, so that what begins as waves becomes, upon reaching the tympanic membrane, vibrations that trip across the ossicles—hammer, anvil, stirrup—toward the cochlea and then on to the millions of microscopic hairs that perform their own conversions, remaking the vibrations into the electrical nerve signals that can be interpreted by the brain. Everything has its translation. Everything can be judged, good or bad. Every sound can tell a story.

But listening is something else. Listening is trying to forget who you are and what you think you need to know so that you can be, really be, inside the church of another's memories. When I listen to Bill tell the many stories of his grandfather, I am tantalized by the possibility of possession, transference. I am persuaded into imagining my own inclusion in his past, into imagining that I can hand these stones of history to our son.

$\mathcal{T}$he facts, as I have said, are elusive, fragile. It is Don Alberto's youngest child, Bill's aunt Adela, who helps me scoop them out, though there are gaps that she herself might find startling and oppressive if she—if any of them—gave the naked facts much weight. In letters she reports on what she supposes matters most, and when I receive them and read them it's as if she were standing here herself with all her elegant height and charming English malapropisms, with the two copper coins of her eyes stitched wide open with mascara. Adela is a smoker and a gossip, and she trusts her English more than her three sisters and one brother do, trusts her rendition of her father's life, her way of translating him through time. She doles him out, memory by memory, photo by photo, so I receive him in no order—he is

young in March and old in May, and by September he is only
young again, sitting in a jail cell, waiting for his execution. When
I ask her to begin at the beginning, she writes, *My great-grandfather was Italian. My grandfather was born in Santa Tecla. My grandmother was born in Santa Tecla. She was of Spanish heritage.*

And then, four sentences in, she is on to the land and its
precursors, which will define most everything going forward.
She is reporting on the progression of near-misses and revivals
and inventions and deals that culminated in Don Alberto's St.
Anthony's Farm. He traded on everything he was in order to get
the land he wanted, repeatedly salvaged his own life so that he
could live it. He was twenty-seven when, still that army captain
of the brass-buttoned jacket and gleaming saber, of my husband's
face, and son's, he took part in a military coup against Jorge
Meléndez, El Salvador's reigning dictator. The year was 1922,
and Don Alberto conspired, REVOLTED FOR DEMOC-
RACY, Adela writes, typing the words in all capital letters so
that I'll understand their implications. He revolted on behalf of
the landless campesinos, she says, on whose backs the country's
crops were harvested, and whose repression was a festering sore,
a prelude to the *matanza*, the coming slaughter. Defeated, Don
Alberto found himself in jail, on trial, scheduled to die by an
executioner's hand, before a firing squad, echoing the legacy
passed on by his great-uncle. "He was scheduled to die?" I write
back. "Really? Don Alberto?" "Yes," Adela answers. "I have
proof." But after waiting for more, I finally ask Bill whether it's
true about his grandfather and the almost execution.

"Yes," Bill says. "He was betrayed by a military friend."

"A friend betrayed him?"

"Yes. He turned him in."

"And so what happened?"

"Years later, after my grandfather was free, he met up with the man again."

"What did he do?"

"My grandfather was rich. The man was homeless." Don Alberto gave him money.

In El Salvador, what people you know and how you know them can overturn most any fate, verdict, sentence. Scheduled to die, Don Alberto had his sentence commuted when a friend with insider connections intervened on his behalf. Scheduled to live out many years in jail, he was in fact released when, in 1923, the dictator Alfonso Quiñónez Molina succeeded the dictator Meléndez, and Don Alberto's father, through yet another secret insider, found a friendly ear. At twenty-eight, with neither uniform nor standing, Bill's grandfather was released from jail and transferred to house arrest in a town called La Libertad. Here he began his life again, making the money that he'd continually leverage until he could buy St. Anthony's Farm. *They were afraid he'd make another GOLPE,* Adela writes, meaning they feared he'd incite another revolt against the military. *So he couldn't leave that town for three years.*

Today La Libertad is a place consumed by itself, a cheap beach haven overpowered by graffiti, street vendors, the idle poor, the vacationers who still kid themselves that the ocean offers sanctuary. Palm trees push up through abandoned buildings. Children sleep in the back of cars. The smoke of tortilla grills rises up from the street corners, and the shards of gunfire-exploded concrete pavilions lie precisely where they fell, deflated beach balloons fitting like grout between the pieces. Out on the dock, women in dirty white dresses sleep beside their stacks of salted fish, and men dye their two-day-old snapper red, making a thief's suggestion of freshness. All the while, urchin children climb in and out of the cracked wooden boats that have been winched down into the Pacific and then hauled back up, where they dry in the sun and serve as trade posts: lobsters, crayfish, crab, turtle, octopus, shark in exchange for a merchant's few colones. The first time I visited La Libertad, Bill walked me out on the long crowded dock and pointed to where he knew the whirlpools were. *A child drowned here,* he pointed. *And there. And between here and that distance is where my grandfather swam, and it was somewhere over there where he nearly died.* When Bill was a kid, he could see the fins of sharks cutting through the frothing breakers like a surgeon's steady knife, and the sharks are still there, as is the powerful undertow, as are the disintegrating bones of the dead.

El Salvador's rivers lead to the Pacific. Anything from the top of a mountain can end up here: Chlorox bottles, feces, a ragged dress that washed away during laundry time at the rocks; the buoyant fish heads from the fisherman's trade float by as well. The beach itself is black with volcanic sand and infested, during some seasons, with massive flying ants that vibrate and twitch across its surface. It's the bigness of the yellow-capping waves that suggests that God is still at work. It's the massive size of the abandoned structures, the very length of the dock that suggests what La Libertad, in Don Alberto's time, actually was.

Located seventeen miles south of Santa Tecla, down a narrow, accident-prone strip of highway, La Libertad, once called Oak Mountain by ancient tribes, opened as a port in the mid-1800s, after the government infused the lonely beachfront with construction funds and made the road to San Salvador at least partly passable. El Salvador's first steamboat glittered in these waters in 1854. In 1857, multinational troops, twelve hundred soldiers strong, departed from there to evict the American

William Walker from Nicaragua. Ten years later, the solid iron wharf went up, and by the time Don Alberto, having been spared his own execution, arrived in 1923, La Libertad was a bustling place, coffee and sugarcane and cattle going out, Europe and the other Americas coming in, in the form of cotton goods, iron and steel, trucks, automobiles. The former army captain had nothing but time. He built PANGAS, Adela writes. Little wooden fishing boats. He rented them for two and a half colones a day. Soon he was using his swimming to his advantage—stroking his way out to where the big cargo ships anchored and getting paid to inspect the quality and honesty of imports. He fought the whirlpools and he won. He stowed his money in quiet safekeeping and dreamed of the jungle above El Limón.

*M*eanwhile, El Salvador was headed toward a holocaust that few Salvadorans mention, even today, at so many decades' distance. Bill says it wasn't taught in schools, when he was growing up. Adela's letters circle, bypass, ignore. History books blithely avert their eyes, making preposterous claims about peace. "Today El Salvador, though the smallest of the Central American republics, is a progressive, energetic country dotted with busy villages," concludes one history, circa 1943. "Except for a brief period in 1906, it has enjoyed years of peace and has used them to develop its many resources."

But in fact, this tiny, volcano-ridden episode of geology and time has brewed misery and war for thousands of years. It was the land, always, standing at the heart of the trouble, the land with a mind of its own. El Salvador is gorgeous, exotic, fertile, ripe, dangerously distributed above fault lines. It inspired, from the beginning, greed; provoked—and heralded—perpetual hope and dissatisfaction. On January 22, 1932, as Don Alberto was finally emerging as a free and independent man, a future coffee baron, El Salvador's most famous volcano, Izalco, blew. His molten, gas-charged rocks spat high into the air, plumed riotously, lathered back down his trembling cone, and kept on pluming. A few hours later, catching the light of Izalco's fire on the blades of their machetes, Indians would be seen streaming over hills and ravines, intent on revolution, on claiming back what had been taken from them, by one perpetrator or another, for thousands of years: decent and liberated lives. They would storm telegraph offices and police barracks, set homes ablaze, machete victims down, serially rape the wives of government officials, even drag an Italian philanthropist to his death. Erupting in the west, the revolt erupted as well in La Libertad and in the leafy neighborhoods of Santa Tecla, where Don Alberto was, by then, rebuilding his life. Within two days, under the leadership of Maximiliano Hernández Martínez (otherwise known as El Brujo, the sorcerer), the Indian uprising would be arrested. For weeks, even months afterwards, there'd be murderous reprisals. By the time the *matanza* was over, an estimated thirty thousand Indians would be dead—all those found carrying machetes, all those heard speaking Nahuatl, all those of Indian features or dress presumed guilty, rounded up, lashed by the thumbs to those rounded up beside them, and shot, sometimes by firing squads that took no pleasure in precision, sometimes by machine guns mounted upon trucks. There was no room, in El Salvador, for all those dead. The bodies rotted in the streets, in drainage ditches. Pigs, buzzards, dogs, flies—it was the smells and the sound of the crunching bones that the few who would speak of it later remembered, it was how they couldn't tell, when they visited their butchers, what was human and what was pork. Izalco, for his part, remained angry and tempestuous long afterwards, his fires lighting the night sky with eerie insistence.

*T*here had been tensions from the beginning—tensions since the Maya had come and settled, more tensions after the Nahuatl swept in, insinuating their own mix of customs, their own religion, dress, their maguey, from which they brewed alcoholic ritual drinks and wove colorful, appealing garments. The Nahuatl supplemented their diet of game and fish with the vitamins of chile peppers and herbs. They extracted balsam from their trees, slicing incisions into the hard balsamo trunks, setting fires about their bases, and pressing wads of cotton below the incisions to catch the bleeding sap. The Nahuatl handed their history down through song and story, not books, and they sacrificed a child every summer to ensure a healthy season of maize, all the while dominating or absorbing competing Indian tribes, imagining, no doubt, that the future belonged to them. They put their own to work as slaves on communal plots of earth. By the time the brutal, blue-eyed Spaniard Pedro de Alvarado arrived on June 18, 1524, the kingdom of Cuzcatlán was a thriving, independent nation. There were political divisions, there were chiefs, there were glorious swaths of cacao orchards on the sides of the massifs, and there was, of course, the endless reconfiguring of the land: brooks erupting into rivers; earthquakes shaking down structures, trees; green fields overflowing with viscous lava and then again giving rise to greenness; volcanoes holding their lamps out in the night.

With his coats of mail, his firearms, his men on horses, his pretensions, Alvarado came so that his country might someday rule, and by 1540, and for three hundred uneasy, unstable years, Spain, incorporating El Salvador into the Spanish Captaincy

General of Guatemala, did. The Nahuatl were vassalized, Christianized, marginalized, devastated by herds of ill-mannered, crop-trampling Spanish cattle, decimated by endemics and plagues—smallpox, measles, yellow fever, typhoid—that they'd never seen before and could not cure. If the Spanish crown prohibited the conquistadores from owning the land outright, it encouraged the creation of encomiendas, plots of land upon which indigenous labor could be demanded in exchange for their Christian "education."

The Indians battled back—learned not to fight in open plains, learned how to roll massive boulders down steep inclines to crush encroaching Spanish soldiers, learned when to retreat, when to attack. But the Spanish persisted, settled down on communal Indian land; introduced the orange, lemon, lime, quince, melon, pomegranate, pineapple, peach to the soil that had known only beans, maize, chile peppers, tobacco, cacao. They planted the earth with sugarcane. They traded balsam, herbs, silver, gold, stolen Indian treasures through the pack mule trains and human cargo bearers that traversed those lands. Increasingly, they converted Cuzcatlán into indigo, a crop whose production and milling was a filthy, disease-ridden enterprise.

Daring to trust their own supremacy, the Spaniards, in El Salvador, built their capitals on noisy, opinionated land: at least six times, between 1545 and 1798, earthquakes shook the capital cities to the ground. Crops failed. Insects stung. The earth refused to yield all that was demanded, and the unabated epidemics and civil unrest so dramatically thinned the native ranks that by 1578 a mere 77,000 of El Salvador's original 500,000 inhabitants survived; by the close of the sixteenth century, just 10,000 Indians could be counted.

In the end, however, it was Spain herself, land-induced greed, that proved to be the colony's most deleterious challenge—a succession of trade-stifling, poverty-inducing royal decrees that heightened unrest across Central America and finally resulted in a revolt against the crown. It was Mexico that led the way to liberation; Central America's independence as a single political entity was declared in Guatemala City in 1821. Then, on June 29, 1823, El Salvador, Guatemala, Honduras, Costa Rica, and Nicaragua broke with Mexico and declared their own independence.

But even this unity would prove illusory, temporary, as, almost immediately, the provinces went to war among themselves. By 1839, the Central American union was null and void. El Salvador formally emerged as an independent state—a *patria*—in 1841. Conflict, coups, invasions from neighboring countries, questions about regional unity, and fears of being absorbed and dominated by Guatemala all marked its early years, as did increasing concerns about its prime export, indigo. *Broad tracts of land have been thrown out of cultivation; some valuable estates have been almost ruined, many entirely so; the buildings, tanks for the manufacture of indigo, and other appurtenances, have become dilapidated or maliciously destroyed by the blind fury of party spirit, or suffered decay, owing to the insecurity consequent to conflicts so destructive,* worried one observer of the time. El Salvador, post independence, was in need, once again, of a miracle.

It arrived, so the story goes, as coffee seeds in the pockets of a Brazilian schoolteacher named Antonio J. Coelho, who had not, apparently, wanted to leave his morning brew behind. It wasn't that coffee hadn't been seen before on El Salvadoran land; rumors and reports of its existence go back to the beginning of the century. It was that Coelho seemed to recognize coffee's commercial potential, and out in the suburbs of San Salvador, on a farm he named La Esperanza, he planted his seeds and nurtured his tenderlings and taught his students the secrets of the shrubby tree. Word spread and so did the trees—first to previously uncultivated lands, then into fields once sown with cereals, fruits, or indigo, or given over to cattle. By 1858, there was legislation in the books freeing all those involved with the cultivation of coffee from public and military service. There were new import/export laws, new public relations campaigns, new politics designed to elevate El Salvador's position in the international economy. Peasants and entrepreneurs alike responded—planting the tenderlings on idle community plots, or renting the land from ethnic communities, or buying stretches of earth for themselves. By the 1880s, local agricultural boards, funded by the state, were giving tens of thousands of coffee trees away for free to those who promised to cultivate the crop. Land laws were being rewritten (and in many indigenous communities angrily protested) to help speed the privatization of what had once been village communal lands. Migrant workers—from Guatemala, from El Salvador's own struggling peasant class—were being called upon to support the farms during the labor-intensive seasons. Aggressive coffee optimism aggressively reshaped the land, aggressively reconfigured places like Santa Tecla, which was converted from an underutilized forested stretch of occasional haciendas into an ambitious coffee center in just a decade's time.

But if Salvadorans needed reminders that they would never, in the end, subjugate the land, that the land was new and perpetually undecided about its own form and generosity, there were terrifying, exotic signifiers. Earthquakes continued to send shockwaves into cities, into the hills. Volcanoes continued to illuminate the sky. Coffee grew slow on the trees. And in 1880, a seismic disturbance at Lake Ilopango proved once and for all that nothing in El Salvador would ever be wholly certain. As townsfolk bore gape-jawed witness, Ilopango began to fill, then overflow. Higher and higher the lake rose until it was spilling into the Jiboa River, killing the fish, frightening onlookers. Now the river was a raging torrent, and the lake itself was slurped away, emptied out, left a full 34 feet lower than it had been just two months before. In the center of the lake, there then appeared an island, a geological apparition rising from the waters. Eventually the island would stack itself to a height of some 170 feet. Eventually the lake would fill back up with fish.

*W*hen you are looking through history for bridges, you find them. When I am looking for ways to conjure up Don Alberto, to will myself into my husband's legacy so that I can yield it more completely to our son, I return again and again to the years just before the *matanza,* to the years when Bill's grandfather dreamed about the land up in the hills. He'd been arrested for rebellion and spared and lived out his incarceration, building and renting *pangas* under house arrest. He spent his hours outside, under the sun, beside the sea, swimming from the dock to the cargo ships, free-stroking back to the wharf, avoiding the whirlpools when he could. What he finally bought with the colones he'd stowed was a chunk of La Libertad itself. He called it AMAQUILCO, Adela writes. It wasn't much, the smallest plot, not enough, certainly, to grow coffee on. It wasn't an end in itself, only a means, something to be leveraged later. Still, it seems to me that Amaquilco stands as proof of Don Alberto's confidence in the life that lay ahead.

It's Don Alberto's optimism in the future that I keep coming up against. His determination to believe in a country that had scheduled his own execution, a nation rarely at peace with the earth beneath its feet. For if it is true that the coffee industry had, by the 1920s, finally come into its own, it is also equally and obviously true that a crisis was mounting. Coffee requires picking, by hundreds of honest hands, but for only three months of the year. It requires certain economies of scale, best achieved, in the eyes of a powerful elite, when historically communal lands are privatized. It requires certain privileges and protections. Coffee, in El Salvador, had given rise to money, urban centers, Packards, Pierce Arrows, European comforts, a conservative ruling class, a national guard whose primary concern was protecting the coffee from its pickers. It had also created a migrant class, exacerbated long-standing social dislocations, discriminations, injustice. Between the *ladino* and the Indian, the oligarchy and the peasant, those who profited and those who made the profit possible, things were coming to a head. Communism was leaking in. And the world at large was on the brink of a massive, excoriating depression.

And yet Don Alberto did not falter. These are the facts, as Adela tells them to me. *When he could leave La Libertad, he sold Amaquilco,* she writes. *With the money he bought first one house and then a second in Santa Tecla. He married my mother. He got a job with the BANCO SALVADOREÑO and then another job with INTERNAL REVENUE. All this time he was saving his money. Finally, when he could, he bought his first bit of land above El Limón. And soon he had his farm up in the hills.*

Nicha

HOME

⌘⌘⌘

$\mathcal{T}$he road to the farm lies deep within two walls of earth. It's been carved out over time, leaving the roots of the shorn trees miserably suspended in midair and the shacks along the edge in a perilous perch. Every time a bus lumbers up or a jeep slides down this road, dust flies—graying the foliage, smacking up against the cardboard hovels, mixing in with the corn meal the women knead with the hands they haven't washed in who knows how long, sifting over and settling in with the rolled *petates,* the paper flowers, the table altars, the plastic saints, the day's wet laundry, the corn husks that will later clean the household's small collection of spoons. Dogs are everywhere, their ribcages so pronounced it seems you could fold them and unfold them, like so many old accordions, and the strays will follow whatever drives by, yelping and sniping alongside, jumping in and out of sight as the wheels hit the ruts and the passengers fly up and down. It's a one-way road, but everything jerks into two directions—the jeeps, the buses, the dogs, the pedestrians, the pickup trucks in which the people stand, their hands against their mouths and eyes, against the storm of dust. Up the mountain takes you, and the road is a crater, wide and deep, and the dogs yelp and the children stare and the roadside cardboard houses stand their ground, the bottlecaps that are used as wash-ers to keep the cardboard from tearing rattling with the din. Don't try to talk; it has to happen to you—the sudden views of El Salvador proper, the equally sudden submergence inside the jungle growth, the banging of heads and elbows and cameras and knees inside the stripped-to-nothing jeep.

The first time I visited St. Anthony's Farm, it was May and sticky hot, and I was somewhere between angry and amazed, one among aunts, maids, brothers in the back of a jeep that squeezed in its passengers face to face, on two abbreviated cushions. In the back of a jeep on a road in a country that was beset by civil war; already thousands upon thousands had died over land such as the land we were driving on. Since there was no trunk and no floor space, wares and provisions were stacked up high on laps, piled on by the maids who'd climbed in last. Bill's aunt Ana Ruth was hunkered down in front, behind the wheel, and my best guess soon became that she'd plotted a multiple murder-suicide.

She had something she wanted me to see, that's all I knew, and under the pressure of her eager foot, the jeep was hurtling forward, down offshoots of the main dirt road, which had hardly been much of a road to begin with. These offshoot roads were oxcart roads, twisted, narrow, pocked, impervious to the needs of machines. They demanded, I concluded, the unwavering precision of a naval pilot returning his aircraft to a ship.

But no. Ana Ruth was in the cockpit and she was giddy with some story, some memory that she was spewing out in Spanish and that was rushing by all naked and untranslated for me. Time and again, she turned around to make her point, to look into the eyes of her audience. Time and again, she lifted both hands and snapped her fingers to add fresh tempo to her tale. Time and again, I looked to Bill, who raised his hand as a way of saying he couldn't interpret now, but maybe—maybe—

he would tell me later. Branches swished by, weeds, and, increasingly, frankly open vistas, where it was all too easy to see just how far up the cliff we were, how casually and dangerously off-balanced, within inches of tumultuous air. When the jeep hit a rock or its wheels left the ground, my companions shrieked amusement-park shrieks, made funny mock-horror faces, then picked the story back up where they had left it, all of it: the hilarity, the snapping fingers, the thicket of Spanish, the riotous relationship with danger. Our knees banged against each other's knees. The pots, the pans, the Tupperware of onions, tomatoes, tortilla, fried chicken ricocheted about us freely. The jeep took the road like an amateur mogul skier, and down we flew, in only approximate parallel to the edge of the crusty cliff. "Look," I finally shouted, over the din of the jeep, the deafening Spanish. "Get her to slow down. I'm walking. Let me out."

"Walking?" Bill shouted back, after my words had finally reached him. He was sitting right beside me, but there was the barrier of noise. "You're not *walking*. Walking isn't safe. Not here."

"Isn't *safe*?" I glared at him as if he alone had carved the roads and personally scrimped on their width. "Are you calling *this* safe?"

"Safer than walking. Especially for you, an American woman."

I considered the country's legacy of war, the purported lawlessness, the purported hatred the campesinos had for the supersonic jets and millions of American dollars that were at work against their cause. Then I caught another flash of all that height rushing by, another wave of nausea as the jeep skidded and shuddered and kept on hurtling. "I don't even know where we're going," I shouted. "Just get her to slow down. I'm walking. Let me out."

"They want you to see how the women wash," Bill shouted back, after the longest while, after he'd apparently weighed in his mind the respective merits and demerits of ruining the surprise.

"What?"

"In the river. It's laundry day. They thought you'd want to take some pictures of the peasant women washing."

"We're risking our lives to see laundry?" I shouted. "*Laundry?*" With an emphatic fist, I struck the nearest Tupperware lid and began to say what I was thinking about the place of peril in frivolous road trips, only to be cut short by the whole new variety of shriek that was now emanating from Ana Ruth herself. The jeep popped, wheeled, spun to a perilous stop, croaked silent. We hung suspended in a volume of dust. The road ahead, when we could finally see it, was but half the width of the jeep. Snapping her fingers and probably cursing, Ana Ruth threw back her head and yanked the keys. There was no going forward, that much was clear, and I couldn't imagine that there was any going back. An election ensued, a rapid vote, a translated headline: Bill was the newly designated pilot. Places were traded. Keys exchanged hands. Now up in front, in Ana Ruth's cockpit, Bill promised, bilingually, to three-point turn the jeep and get us back to the top of the hill. Nothing but narrowness and cliff, but this was the plan. And no one was letting me out.

This is great, I thought to myself. Just great. I'm going to die. I'm going to die in a rumble of dust in a plummet through green because it's laundry day in El Limón.

I don't remember much about how we got back up that road, save for the generally sincere nature of all the screaming. I do remember the reflected fraction of my husband's face in the rearview mirror, the joy he seemed to take in extricating the jeep beast from its jungle troubles. Daring gravity, badgering the edge, gaining traction in the loose, gravelly dust, he held the very landscape in his grip, the imperfect restless assertive nature of his grandfather's farm. He had told me before how he had loved the challenge of those roads. *I was fourteen. My grandfather taught me. He let me drive us everywhere.* But he had told me this in Philadelphia, where we together lived and where I had lived for most of my life, making my understanding of roads and driving somehow impervious to his tales. He had told me this with his impeccable English, with his dark eyes looking out over his freckles, over the surprisingly light quality of his skin.

Bill doesn't look as foreign as he is. He has lived here, in the United States, since he left Santa Tecla for college at eighteen, and in a family of Marios and Rodolfos and Albertos, he has a most American name, a name his father pulled out of a novel he was reading one July right before his first son's birth. Besides, he is an architect and an artist, not a farmer, and his education is elite and Ivy League, so I can look at him and think his home is where I am, with me, and I can convince myself that I know what he's suggesting through his tales. But my husband's home is El Salvador, the rhythms of a language I do not speak, the memories of a jungle that could pitch a man to death, the simple, poetic, unexpected idea that what is to be shared and seen on a sunny day is women rubbing the stains out of their clothes on silver river rocks. *And sometimes they take their mules to the river, and sometimes their children play naked on the banks, and from a certain angle, high above, it can look like a mosaic. They bathe themselves when their laundry is done, and then they take the children home.*

My husband isn't home unless he's in El Salvador, unless he's standing in the shadows of Don Alberto's land. Unless he's feeling the kick of the Pacific on his face, or asserting the privileges of a machine on jungle roads, or walking beside the gardener who knew him as a boy, and who today, nearing his eightieth birthday, still fetches coconuts from trees, still shares his secrets. My husband isn't home unless he's speaking Spanish, but when he first took me to El Salvador, less than a year into our marriage, I saw danger instead of beauty, and I felt fear. I saw all that would always keep us separate and strange, and I felt alone, as I'd never felt before. Bill said I should stop thinking, weighing, worrying, distrusting. That I should look around with different eyes and see the good that he'd come from.

That first day on St. Anthony's Farm, Bill proved that he too was capable of miracles, that he, like his grandfather, has the fine knack of survival. Bearing an armor of soft dust, scattering the parakeets in the trees, sending loose gravel over the cliff's edge instead of us, the jeep, under Bill's care, made it home, made it, in other words, to a clearing, high up, to a sensible, flat, and, again, dusty place that long ago had been chosen for its view. It's here that St. Anthony's Farm gives way to open space and structure—to two narrow rectangles that face each other across a denuded courtyard.

On the left is the house—squat, red brick, Spanish roof tiles, big doors, barred-in windows, completely lacking in monied pride—that Don Alberto built for himself, for living in during the height of coffee season. On the right, nearly identical, is the house where the cooks, the maids, the administrators have, in respectful succession, lived. In the middle is a stony grotto, and above the grotto rises a mangled, big-leafed *papaturro* tree, and we climbed it, Bill and I, after that first road trip was over, after the maids and the aunts and the brothers and Bill's mom had relieved the jeep of its cascaded Tupperware.

There are hardly any photographs of Bill and me together, but that day someone snapped a picture of the two of us straddling the *papaturro* tree. We have the same light skin and freckles, the same dark hair and eyes, the same slight build, different expressions. We might be confused for brother and sister, save that one of us is looking out, and the other's looking in. Bill was telling me, I remember this, that I was sitting in his spaceship. That this was the place that he'd go as a kid when he wanted to circle the moon. *Imagine that,* I remember Bill saying to me. *Imagine sitting here and taking off for the moon.* And the look on my face suggests what is true: I am working hard to see.

We grow into what we trust, what we are willing to believe. The stories like seepage, the past brought forward, the edges blurred but not dissolved. Bill began telling me the stories of St. Anthony's Farm during our first afternoon together, after a softball game in Philadelphia in July of 1983, and in 1986, during the month of May, I sat, now his wife, in a *papaturro* tree and saw for myself how imperfectly the facts had been translated by my imagination. I'd read books, studied photographs, listened to Bill at night, and asked questions, but St. Anthony's Farm had little to do with the farm that I'd conjured in my head. I'd placed Bill's childhood in a landscape of my own making, ascribed the gentleness of Pennsylvania dairy farms to a terrain of jagged pitches. I'd made the footpaths wide enough for pack mules, caravans, side-by-side horses. I'd assumed the coffee trees were generously trunked, and widely spaced—had imagined taking a book out among them and propping myself up beneath the shade. I had listened, and I had gotten it wrong, and now I was out on a limb with Bill, in a *papaturro* tree that was also a spaceship, that was also a memory of flying to the moon.

In a while lunch was served, the jeep party reconvening for a meal at the table that had been stealthily set within the slender open porch of Don Albertos's red brick house. White linen. Polished silver. Bill's brothers: Mario, Rodolfo, but not Bill's father; the divorce had been finalized, quietly, a few years before.

Bill's mother, Nora, and her sisters: Ana Ruth, Martha, Adela. Friends of the family. The maids—Nicha and Selena—in their blue-and-white checked uniforms. And plantains and black beans and the chicken roughly chopped in quarters, fried. A bowl of diced onions. A bowl of diced tomatoes. Tortillas arriving hot from across the courtyard, from a kitchen black with fifty years of tortilla fires and a Maya tradition, thousands of years old. They came on a polished sterling silver tray that was carried by a dusty, barefoot boy. The Spanish was slower than it had been in the jeep. The stories were somehow more restful. I stopped dividing the sounds into syllables, stopped trying to assert my own understanding, stopped questioning, stopped hoping Bill would translate, finally, relievedly, stopped hearing. I looked out beyond the porch toward the jungle of the trees, caught specks of color—butterflies? birds?—up in the leaves. It was a hot day. My tongue was heavy with dust. I noticed the barefooted boy cutting another path across the courtyard, toward our table. Noticed how the sun flamed the silver tray and how the tortilla smoke exhaled a cloud above the pitch-black kitchen. I had been exiled from all that I knew, and my husband was home.

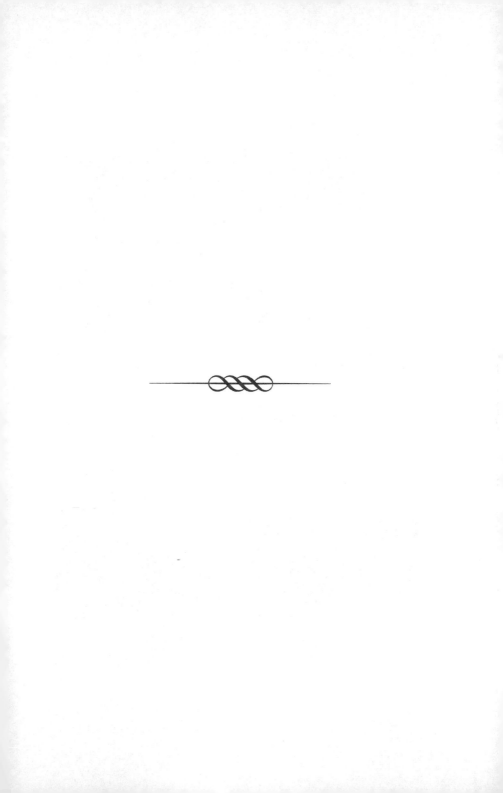

Afternoon at the farm

ST. ANTHONY

———∞∞∞———

*I*t was St. Anthony who persuaded an ass to leave its stable
and kneel before the sacrament, or so the story goes, St. Anthony
who saved a field of corn from hungry birds. This was the man
who flawlessly memorized Scripture, who orated dramatically,
whose very charisma seduced others to believe. This was the
man who became the patron saint of the poor and the
oppressed, of barren women, harvests, of Padua and Flemish
men. "Lost things," Bill says, when I ask him what St. Anthony
promises to redress. Invoke him, wear his medal at your neck,
keep his likeness in your pocket, and you will find what has disappeared.

   You will come upon St. Anthony in paintings in galleries
with a lily in his hand, or books, or a tiny baby Jesus. And sometimes the ass is there, and sometimes fish, and inevitably he
wears the simple heavy robes of a Franciscan monk. On the
mantel in our house, he stands barefooted on a pedestal, ten
impressive inches tall, shedding the dark blue paint of his
ceramic coat and raising his right hand in greeting. His left hand
has to be imagined, for it is gone, as is the greater percentage of
his black halo-ing hair, and his right cheek is endangered by a
hairline crack that extends from the lower ledge of his painted
lashes to the top of his black-lipped mouth. No one knows

where our St. Anthony came from; Bill suggests that he's one hundred years old.

When I look at him now minding our quiet suburban living room, I remember that first day on the farm, the hours after the meal, the early afternoon, when the party took its siesta while the maids washed the dishes clean, and I sat feeling in exile. Everyone had found a place to sleep—two to three on each inside bed, two outside sharing a hammock—but I wasn't going to go to sleep, and so, out of respect for me, neither was Bill. I needed to hear English again. I needed explanations. I needed the stories told once more, the questions answered, so that I could imagine them now in their context. "Why St. Anthony?" I wondered out loud. "Of all the possibilities, of all the saints, why name the farm for him?" We had climbed back up into the tree, and I was wearing a camera. We were facing one another, longing for a breeze.

"Lost things," Bill said.

"Was your grandfather religious?"

"He says he was, before I knew him."

"And when you knew him?"

"No. He hardly went to church. He was angry at the priest of the Church of St. Anthony, and he stayed that way, long as I knew him."

"Angry for what?"

"For not coming out to the farm for the peasants, even after he'd given that priest's church a lot of money, even though it was his money, mostly, that had financed the construction of St. Anthony's Church in Santa Tecla. My grandfather asked the priest to come to the farm and serve the peasants once a year, and the priest flat-out refused."

"So what did Don Alberto do?"

"He persuaded the priest from the Church of St. Carmen to come. He asked him and he paid him, and in that way he still managed to give the peasants their St. Anthony's Day. But the church for him, after that, was always a hypocrite. And he never gave another peseta to St. Anthony's Church in Santa Tecla."

I looked out then over the peaceful courtyard and tried to see the St. Anthony's Day that Bill began conjuring up for my sake, because I'd asked him. The peasants flocking toward the clearing from all directions on the hill—from their one-room huts and shacks, from their cardboard enclosures pinned together with bottle caps. Wearing shoes if they had shoes, wearing their finest Sunday clothes, which were torn, perhaps, or grease stained, but always scrubbed as clean as rocks and river water make clothes clean, and pressed creaseless with patient hands. They came up the hill and down the hill, turned at the rickety metal gate and pooled between the two brick houses in the clearing above the farm, where flags of colored paper had been hung and benches pulled out into the sun. Beneath the low-slung porch, Don Alberto had covered a table with a white linen cloth and made an altar, and there this priest, this Father Ascue, had arranged the accoutrements of God: the cross, the chalice, the host, St. Anthony, too, an imposing two feet tall.

When it was time, when the peasants had filled the narrow porch and spilled out into the courtyard, when the sun had dissipated the chill of the morning, when Bill himself, or a brother, or a cousin, had taken his place beside Father Ascue in his own best Sunday clothes, the mass began. Behind his altar, Father Ascue stood: intoning, instructing, condemning, forgiving, pausing now and again for María López, who would sing all the right hymns in their right order.

"María López?"

"Yes. Old as long as I knew her. White hair. Lived down the road in a shack on my grandfather's farm. Knew every word of every hymn."

"Did she stand?"

"What?"

"When she sang?"

"No. She kneeled on the side of the porch in the same pink dress year after year, and she sang with this flat nasal voice, this almost comical voice, like the sound of slang. But she wasn't to be mocked, my grandfather made this clear, and she was famous because she knew the words, and when the others knew the words, they'd sing along with her, and my mother and my grandmother: they'd sing too."

"How did she know all the words?"

"Who?"

"María López?"

"I don't know. Nobody asked her. She just did."

"Okay." I looked toward the porch where the only sign of the meal we'd just eaten was a black bird, pecking crumbs off the hard cinnamon-colored tile. I imagined a little white-haired lady in a thin pink dress on her knees among the benches, her hands enclasped, her eyes closed tight as she belted out her hymns. I tried to imagine my husband at the altar, but I knew him too well, or thought I did.

When it came time for the first communions, the kids swelled forward—the girls like so many brides in white dresses and long veils, the boys in their white shirts and navy pants, all the tongues going out for the host Father Ascue held above them. And the parents and the brothers and the sisters and the others sat on the benches, stood in the sun, looked on, witnessed the blessings of the children.

"You'd see the same kids, year after year, making their first communions," Bill said. He was looking toward the jungle while I still looked out across the courtyard.

"The same kids?"

"The first communion kids didn't just get blessed. They got my grandmother's candy. That was mostly the point, at least for them."

"So they kept coming back?"

"Yes. They had several first communions each."

"That's funny."

"It was funny. But it was also sweet. It was . . . ," Bill stopped, exhaled. "It was really something."

"I'm sure."

"And you know what?"

"What?"

"It doesn't happen anymore. It's gone. St. Anthony's Day died with my grandfather."

After the kids got the wafers on their tongues, and turned around and smiled back out at their families on the benches in the sun, those who wanted to get married could—the men and their women, their children at their feet or in their arms, the vows exchanged, the unions sanctified. After that those adults who wanted a blessing and a wafer came, and Father Ascue, alongside St. Anthony, ministered. It ended, Bill remembers, with a María López solo, and then brunch was served out in the courtyard. Tamales from Lenora's kitchen. Sweet white creamy *atol*, which was brewed from corn and ladled out of buckets into the peasants' drinking gourds. Up on the porch, meanwhile, a table was set for Don Alberto and his family and for Father Ascue, the St. Carmen priest who had come because the St. Anthony's priest had refused. The meal arrived in pots and on trays, in the hands of well-groomed maids: a vegetable soup thickened with chunks of plantain, a slab of burnt steak, a strip of salted meat, chickens soaked in onions, milk cheese, sweet breads, the farm's own coffee for dessert. They'd eat until they hurt, until the peasants had dispersed, until the adults, including the priest, went inside for their siesta. Bill and his brothers and his cousins: they didn't sleep. They went out behind the tortilla kitchen and climbed the fruit trees: tangerine, orange, lime, and sometimes mango, though these are the hardest trees to climb.

"You were hungry after all that?"

"No, we weren't hungry. But the fruit was sweet. And we just hung out there, smoked cigarettes, talked, whatever, waiting for the fiesta."

"The fiesta?"

"It began at night. We had to wait until dusk had fallen." And then Bill remembered what more he could remember, and I, as best I could, picked up the trail of that memory. Imagined the clearing between rectangular houses gone abruptly black with nightfall, and the peasants, having gone home and tended their laundry and their chickens and their weedy strips of garden and their leaking shacks, now returning in their Sunday bests, returning for the St. Anthony's Day fiesta. Up the rugged hills they come, a smattering of candles in their hands, the moon floating high above their heads, the stars tossed like so many yellow eyes across the sky. And maybe their shoes are hung about their necks, and maybe they're singing or maybe telling stories about their child's first communion, or scolding those same children at their sides. When they reach the courtyard, they find a circle of kerosene light, they find the big old pots of *gallo en chicha* that Lenora has been stirring in her kitchen—this thick, creamy rooster-and-potato-and-*chicha* soup that cannot be made until the corn has been boiled and decanted and fermented and decanted and again fermented, then enhanced with the flavors of brown sugar and maguey. It's delicious, I'm told, and it gets you drunk, and it warms up the band from El Limón that has come to play its marimba rhythms at Don Alberto's request. It warms up the peasants who have reconvened from across the hill, and who are eating now, and dancing, laughing, while Don Alberto and his wife and his daughter look on. Closing my eyes now, I think I see it, and so many years ago, in the *papaturro* tree, I thought I'd seen it, too.

"And where are you?" I asked Bill back then, because in my mind's eye he was out in the courtyard, he was dancing. "Where are you?" I wanted to know, that day, in the tree.

"I'm inside my grandfather's house, with my brothers and my cousins," Bill answered. "I'm watching it all go on through the windows, those windows: there." Bill pointed from our post on the *papaturro* tree toward the windows of the rectangular house—no glass there, only bars, like prison bars. I concentrated, hard, and tried to conjure up the fiesta from the vantage point of my husband's childhood—the El Limón band to the left, the pots of stewed rooster to the right, the peasants in cotton pinks and yellows and blues dancing too close to the kerosene flames and drinking *atol* out of split gourds.

"Why were you inside?" I asked. "Instead of out here, with the party?"

"That was my grandfather's rule. The fiesta was for the peasants. The fiesta was their day, he said. Besides, they all got disgustingly drunk, and it wasn't much of a place for kids."

"So you stayed inside and watched the whole thing through the windows?"

"Not really. We'd sneak out. We'd get some *gallo en chicha*. We'd tease old Santana."

"Santana?"

"María López's husband, from down the hill. He was a crazy drunk, and he could never catch us, but it was fun getting him mad and running away, watching him threaten us from behind. It felt dangerous, but it never really was, because we always beat him, and because we always knew we would."

"So when did it end, St. Anthony's Day?"

"Whenever we got tired, we went to bed, lay there listening to the music from the band of El Limón, to the slang of the peasants of the hill, to my grandfather and my grandmother and my mother laughing, talking, but never laughing about the peasants or their slang; it wasn't tolerated, they were to be respected. In the morning, before anyone else was awake, we'd race down the hill in our pajamas and dive into the old water hole."

"Down the hill?"

"That way."

I turned and looked out to where Bill was looking. Beyond the limbs of the *papaturro* tree, beyond the rim of the dusty courtyard, and down, steeply down, toward the river we could not see but trusted was there, toward the water hole where, once, long before I knew him, Bill and his brothers and his cousins and his friends played, while St. Anthony's Farm and all those who had come to celebrate it slept in the aftermath of the wrong priest's blessing.

Cemetery for the poor

DIVISIONS

———— ∞ ————

*I*t isn't safe in El Salvador. Of this you are repeatedly reminded. You are whispered and gossiped at, stormed with a riot of evidence of civil disturbance, roadside assaults, gunpoint robberies, shocking violations against Americans, especially women. You're told: Be careful. You're told: Beware the risks. You're told: The war goes on and on; there are still reprisals, there's still unrest. And then you're told about the shimmery gorge, way below. About the bougainvillea, way high up. About the little girls with the new batch of puppies who are playing on the other side of the hill. You're told about songs birds will sing at certain hours of the day, about the cinnamon-colored dove and the black robin, about the possibility of ocelots in trees, about the shrine that was built inside the hut down the road, all bits of colored, cracking paper, sun-startled aluminum foil. You're told about fiestas, you are seduced toward the past, and you want to come down on the side of beauty, not danger.

I am not an adventuress. I am not a sophisticate. I am a sub-urban-minded woman from Pennsylvania who looked, for such a long time, like a teen. I am easily stranded in the *papaturro* tree when St. Anthony's wakes after siesta. Stranded with wonder and with English, with the bald, increasingly disturbing fact that the man I married, the man I deeply love, feels no apparent compunction to stop the Spanish to make room for me. When the others sleep, he is mine. When they wake, he is assuredly theirs, translating only when I ask him to, releasing the barest minimum of facts. A half hour of his family's Spanish will go by—a half hour of back-and-forth and rollick and lull and wildly gesticulated sadness, disgust, surprise—and all this Bill will convert into one lonely English sentence, one mutter over his shoulder toward me. So that I'll ask, *What was that?,* at a convenient pause in the commotion. And he'll simply say, *They were telling a story.* And because he doesn't want to lose the next chapter of the Spanish, because he is in fact *part* of the story, he leaves me there, on the outside, with the obvious. I take it personally. Bill says I shouldn't. Spanish is not their act against me. Still. I love the stories that Bill tells about his country. I mind, I feel *abraded,* when the stories aren't reshaped for me. So that danger isn't just the war that will not end. It is the subversion of a marriage.

"Where are you going?" I asked that first day in the *papaturro* tree, after Bill had told his tales about St. Anthony's Day and repeat first communions, about a singer and her husband, the one tone-deaf, the other drunk, after I'd started to imagine that I had seen it for myself, after I'd been lulled into a sweet transplanted moment. The others had begun stirring from their naps, and there was the slow, agitating flutter of Spanish on the porch. It was clear all of a sudden where Bill now felt he had to be. That he'd be putting away his memories and joining his past in present time.

"I'm going over there." He indicated the porch where the aunts, the brothers, the mother, the friends were sitting upright on a scatter of chairs, yawning out the end of sleep, accepting iced gin from the maids.

"Why?" I wanted to know, a sullen question that wasn't so

much a question as a declaration, a statement of fact. It was: *I wish you wouldn't go right now. I wish you wouldn't choose them over me.*

"Why?" Bill repeated what I'd said as a way of not acknowledging what I'd meant. "Because they're there, Beth. Because I want to." He was my husband for just that instant more, speaking to me in our shared language, pretending to be someone I'd thought I understood. Then he jumped from the tree and his feet hit the ground and he was a Salvadoran, speaking Spanish, in a clap of dust. From across the plaza, a wave of rolled *r*'s and harshened *j*'s took him in. I was left with a camera at my neck in the spaceship that had abruptly landed, left with a quick flare of unreasonable anger. Joining Bill on the porch would mean sitting deafly, dumbly while torrents of Spanish flew by. It would mean watching my husband—so quiet, so private, so taciturn in English—dial in to a spontaneity I had never once provoked in him, a full-gut laugh that he'd simply never laughed with me. It wasn't just that he was far more foreign when he was home. It was that he was happier and more alive. That he needed me for nothing then, or nothing I could imagine.

Wanting time to myself before I surrendered to the Spanish, I slid out of the tree and set off across the courtyard and out through the crooked, metal gate, calling to no one in particular that I wasn't going far. I went down the dirt road between the two dug-out walls of earth that towered above my head. Hiking up the road while I was hiking down came two brightly dressed women, their hair the color of ink, their postures accommodating the pitch of the road, as well as the woven baskets in their arms and the plastic water jugs that sat on the *yaguales* upon their heads. One jug was blue, and one was orange, and the women kept their eyes low as they passed, not meeting mine, not inviting inquiry, not keen, I sensed, on my camera.

I hadn't gone far before the dogs found me, an ugly, snarly pack, half starved and probably only partly sane, three or four, maybe, I can't remember. Mongrels. Their coats short, sparse, bristly, as a wild pig's hide, their ears angered flat against their heads. They had nothing between them but their hunger, no reason not to attack the thin, white American girl-woman who had come upon them accidentally and who now stood, grossly transfixed, as they blasphemed her through yellow teeth. I was aware of a broken tree limb on the road. I picked it up. I heeled my way up the incline of the road, holding the stick out before me like some kind of Man of La Mancha warrior. I inched backwards. Jowl to jowl, the dogs howled forwards. I wondered if Bill would hear, if I'd be rescued, if I should turn and run like hell.

But before I could act, I was saved by a barefooted boy who out of nowhere then appeared with a fistful of dog-deterring rocks. He hurled. The dogs scattered. The dogs returned. He hurled again. In the dissipating dust, I gestured my thanks, then half walked, half ran to the place I'd come from. I held the camera tight against my chest. I cursed the country, and I blessed it. I hurried past the gate of St. Anthony's, past a herd of wild chickens, past more women bearing jugs. I kept on walking until I came upon a path cut into the high wall of earth beside the road. The path rose vertically on tight, hard, dirt steps, and it was at the end of this path, as I'd been told, that the peasant dead were laid to rest. I swung my camera unto my back and pulled myself toward them, with my hands.

To be among the dead at St. Anthony's is to enter into communion with wild turkeys. They crowd the open spaces between the haphazard graveyard markers, swallowing hard seeds of earth, wobbling the rubbery apparatus about their necks, above their heads. Black feathered and tall, they look up at you with bored, rheumy-eyed resilience, then return to hammering the dirt bits with their beaks.

The graveyard is at least thirty feet above the main road, on an elevated ledge of earth that takes some getting to—hand over hand, each footstep carefully measured and placed. The ascent seems relentlessly vertical, at a near ninety-degree angle to the road, so that when you reach the top you're breathless and you pause, however briefly, in the rush of vertigo. The cemetery itself is a merciful sprawl, nearly flat, a messy mix of tall, wide-bladed grass and spiny bushes and not particularly pretty shade trees. Plunged like daggers to the ground are the crosses, mainly a fabulous aqua color, though some are bleached white and some are unpainted, and at the heads of some newly turned mounds of earth there is nothing but a block of stone. It looks like the aftermath of a piñata party, with crepe-paper chains strewn like leis about the necks of the gravestone markers, plastic red roses wreathed at the feet, errant scraps of yellow paper and transparent cellophane trapped between the blades of grass. There are no cemetery-style rows or columns, no obvious order. Bodies must be planted every which way in the ground.

The turkeys, apparently, don't mind. They go about their business beneath the unmajestic trees, among new shafts of bamboo and misplaced stalks of corn, beside crosses that bear the evidence of the dead in uneven, hand-carved script. Pedro Osegleo. Eugenio Sorono. An eroded, unreadable name. That day, alone with the turkeys among the dead, I used my camera to take it in. To make me stop and attend to the ordinary details, to the facts of that place, to the markers—so many markers— that bore no name at all. I put the camera between me and the graveyard, perversely, as a way of collapsing the distance.

The sun had started to set, and the road below the cemetery had acquired the glow of wet clay. No jug-headed women just then, no ravished dogs, and it was possible, looking down from where I stood, to imagine a funeral coming. Possible to almost see it rising from the bottom of the hill, small at first, then swelling as neighbors and children and chickens and pigs and whatever else joined in. The road filling with a funeral, and the dust it made obscuring the sky, and the dead man loose in his box, sliding, angled, complaining about the pocks and pitches of the road.

At the diversion that was the cemetery path, I imagined the mourners going single file, yielding the coffin to the strongest arms, to those who could bear its burden up the steep incline, who could keep their footing on the polished, slippery earth stairs beneath the weight of bones and box. It would be work to carry the dead, to heave him up the hill, to transport him to the hole that was likely already dug. And there wouldn't be a priest waiting, and none would be expected, and one among them would stand there with a cross clutched to her breast. And then whatever would be said would be said, whatever would be sung, sung, and the mourners would cover the coffin with dirt, drape a crepe-paper garland across the bed of soil, and in single file— they could leave only in single file—slide back down the path, leaving the turkeys to protect or to thieve, I could not imagine which. I'd have to ask Bill when he returned to the land of my English. When I returned to him.

The sun was setting. I couldn't bear darkness alone. I left the cemetery by way of the narrow, vertical path, my shoes riding me road-ward like a pair of skis. I headed back down the main road and up through the metal gate, where the farm was receding into violet shadows and the gathering at the porch had dissipated. When I found Bill, he was looking out at all that coffee turning purple. "Did you get good pictures?" he wanted to know. I answered, "Maybe. A few." Holding my questions. It was only later, many years later, that Bill told me that it was true, what I'd imagined: that the mourners ascend and descend in single file. And afterwards, Bill said, the party begins. Sometimes they kill the dead man a pig. Chase it from some plot on the side of some hill, wrestle it down, tie it with hemp, hoist it upside down and wailing from the rafters of a campesino's house until its legs break so loud you hear the bones crack, you hear the marrow leaking out.

Bill said this when it was just the two of us, when it was me and him and his impeccable, familiar English, when we were home, in Pennsylvania, safe in our bed. He said that next someone goes and gets a bucket of river water, and into the water they shove the pig's snout. They drown the pig, he said; he'd seen it, when he was a kid. They force the snout into the pail, bristles first. And the pig's lips curl against its teeth, and the tongue lashes out and then the whole pig gives up and goes limp. It's a horrible thing. It's unimaginable, Bill said. The big, bloated defeated pig just hanging from the beam of a poor man's roof. They toss the water out, then. Empty the pail and put it on the ground, directly beneath the suspended carcass. Then someone draws a machete and strikes: a slice across the neck. Blood jewelry.

"And after that, what do they do?"

"They put the pig on a stick above a fire and they turn it and serve it when it's tender."

That first day at the farm, we returned to Nora's house in Santa Tecla, all of us piled back into the jeep and safe with Nora at the wheel, taking the main road up, around, then down. The Tupperware was light as air on our laps, and on either side of me Nicha and Selena closed their eyes, taking their sleep, I supposed, where they found it, keeping their bodies rigid, upright, and neatly to themselves. Dusk had softened the outline of things. Greens were gray. Individual trees were forests. The roadside huts at the bottom of the hill were smoky and indistinct. And the children we passed were filthy with the dust, their eyes radiant.

The living and the dead; the day and the night; the farm and the city; the Spanish and the English: divisions had been established. The next morning I woke in a single bed in a clean white room, the sun pouring its bleach onto all things. On the opposite side of an old night table, Bill lay asleep on his own single bed, perfectly noiseless and still, betraying nothing. Beyond the bedroom door, I could hear Nicha's feet sliding across the white marble floors of Nora's house and the percolating coffee in the kitchen. Sitting up, I tried to read the book I'd brought from home, but all I really wanted was my husband's perfect heat, all I really wanted was to throw back my quilt and journey to his side of the room, kiss his cheek, and then his lips, and settle into the bedsheets beside him, which then I did. He turned toward me as he almost always does. An instinct even stronger than his dreams.

Later, while the family collected at Nora's table for coffee and sweet breads, I slipped out into the walled-in yard. The skirt of a volcano rose beyond the brick walls, clouds smoked harmlessly across an intransigent sky. It was already warm, and the butterflies and bees seemed anxious to get their pollinating done. Tiburcio, the ancient gardener, was peacefully at work, pruning and watering and calculating. He wasn't more than five feet tall. His thin collared shirt had only three remaining buttons; the hem of his khaki pants scuffed against the ground. Tied loosely and poorly with hemp, his pants puckered out around his waist, hung low at the crotch, suggesting the thinnest of legs. On his head Tiburcio wore a cheap Panama hat, a pale wheat color save for the dark hatch marks along the brim. His watch, too big and excessively heavy, dangled loosely past his wrist and toward his hand, toward the ficus and the fern and then the orange tree that he was watering. The garden was an Eden, hemmed in on all four sides by tall brick walls against which pregnant rose bushes pressed their burdened limbs. Flowers I'd never seen before held out bodacious blooms and relinquished themselves to the care of Tiburcio's small brown hands and black, slightly slanted eyes. He moved from plant to tree to bud, attending to each living thing as if it were a child in a school.

Tiburcio is a museum piece in a country that exterminated thousands just like him: dark skin, Indian eyes, the ever-ready sharp machete. "Good morning, Tiburcio," I called, and he nodded. "*Buenos días,*" I said flatly, badly. Another nod. "Your garden is beautiful," I said, and then again he nodded, his slight chin ducking toward his concave chest, his eyes blinking quickly, a gesture of respect, not comprehension, a gesture I returned.

In strangely fashion we then stood silently in the garden, I admiring the things I didn't have names for, and he keeping the names to himself. He was, as Bill had once promised, a genius in the garden, this man who had no garden of his own. He'd been nursing the family's hibiscus and lemon grass and bougainvillea ever since he'd "come with the farm," as they say, by which they mean, after Bill's parents, shortly following their wedding, bought the newlyweds five *manzanas* just up the hill from St. Anthony's, a starter farm, so to speak, a farm called La Esperanza—Coelho's original farm. Tiburcio and his one-room shack and his *comal* and his infamously jealous wife, Lydia, were all part of the package, all part of what the farm's former owners sold to Nora and her husband, Mario, shortly after their wedding day, shortly before my husband was born. So Tiburcio kept his shack, and in exchange he surrendered loyalties—

guarding the five *manzanas* from would-be pests, loafers, assailants; overseeing the planting and picking of coffee; encouraging the tenderlings; pruning the shade trees; and weeding the in-between places clean. In the off-seasons, or on Saturday afternoons, or whenever he was summoned, really, Tiburcio would leave his family and the farm and walk the long, mostly dirt distance to Santa Tecla, to Don Alberto's house, where the garden awaited his care. Roses, Bill has told me: bright reds, bright oranges, yellows. Trees: fig, papaya, tangerine, lemon, orange, banana, and a nut tree, the only one of its sort in the entire country, which grew its yellow, brown, and green nut fruits in mysterious pineapple-like clusters. And after Tiburcio was done with Don Alberto's garden, he'd walk the few blocks to Nora and Mario's home, where the garden was smaller but no less loved by the Indian's hands. *He knows the cure for every spot on every leaf, knows every branch that has to go,* Bill has told me, several times. *He knows what to do to the soil and he knows how to keep the birds away and when he has made his suggestions he has been listened to, because nobody knows gardens like Tiburcio.*

A gentle man, then, who repaired the broken wings of birds, who never made much of the knowledge he had and could machete the skin off an orange in three quick strokes, and who had killed a man, also, and who was a suspected ladies' man, a man from whose roof ledge that slaughtered pig was hung; you could hear the squealing, Bill has said, from way down the road. I won't believe the murder story until it is retold many times— something to do with the defense of Tiburcio's son, a deadly confrontation that took place shortly after Don Alberto's passing. "They say Tiburcio's son had been beat up or harassed," Bill says. "So Tiburcio took it upon himself to straighten things out. He went to the house of the man who'd done the harassing, and he told him the harassing had to stop. The machetes came out, they always do, and Tiburcio's blade sliced through the other man's heart. Went several inches in, they say. Which makes sense. Those blades are sharp."

"Tiburcio stabbed a man in the heart with a machete?" I never do believe it. It seems impossible. Tiburcio's so small. He is a grower of things, not a killer.

"He says it wasn't like that. He says the man fell into his blade."

"Fell into his blade? Do you believe that?"

"It's what he told my mother."

"Was he arrested?"

"The national guard came and took him away. He sat in jail for a couple of years, the one in town, in Santa Tecla. It was painted green, still is. The guards walk around on its roof. You've seen it, don't you remember? We've driven by, walked right past it. It's right in the center of town."

"But what happened after that?" I want to know, and no, I don't remember the jail.

"My mother went to see him. So did the maids, my brothers, sometimes my father. They took him food. They kept him company. My mother, she went almost every week."

"And you?"

"I was in college then, in the States. When I came home, I chose not to go. I thought it would embarrass him, me seeing him like that in a jail. Maybe it wasn't the right thing to do, to not go visit, but that way, between us, between Tiburcio and me, the killing never happened. We never discussed it. He never had to explain it to me."

"When did they let him out of jail?"

"My mother got him out of jail. She knew the mayor, the

judge, the guards, she knew everyone in town and everyone in charge, and she wouldn't let up until they let him go. Then one day Tiburcio was free, but I don't really remember when."

And so Tiburcio returned to his farm, his wife, their slew of kids, returned of course to Nora's garden, where, it is rumored, he began an affair with Nicha, Nora's favorite maid. Nicha's family, like Tiburcio's, had come from a town near El Limón. She had a slew of kids of her own and a husband who was notoriously jealous.

In any case, neither Tiburcio nor Nicha ever admitted to the intrigue, both protested when questions would get asked; both still do. But Lydia, Tiburcio's wife, didn't need proof or a confession. Lydia knew the truth, or so she said, and she despised Nicha for stealing her man's heart; she despised her and she wanted revenge. So, as Bill has said many times, always shaking his head, chortling, smiling, Lydia would wait for Nicha on the side of the road, wait outside Tiburcio's one-room shack, when she knew that Nicha was coming home for weekend visits or holidays. She'd stand there with a stockpile of stones at her feet, and when she saw Nicha coming, she'd hurl—stone after stone, insult over insult. Running to dodge the stones, Nicha would curse old Lydia back, and Tiburcio was stuck between two women's ire.

But was he thinking of any of that while he snapped the flowers clean of their dying leaves in Nora's garden that day? I doubted it then, and I doubt it now. He seemed serene, a perfect complement to the shape and the smell of present time.

*I*t was later that morning that I found the coffee tree Tiburcio had planted in the cloistered city garden. One single coffee tree in the lush, short, sickled grass, and next to it, Nora's birds of paradise. Both of them were set off to themselves, in a crescent-shaped side courtyard that served as a light well for the house. The tree was the picture of elegance, standing there, something sculptural and decorative, and most magnificently out of place. It had been uprooted, it seemed to me. Put down in foreign soil. Made lonely. Coffee trees don't belong in the city, and they don't belong alone.

But then again, they don't belong in El Salvador. Grabbing my camera and slipping through a glass door to the crescent outside, I studied the tree through my lens, clicked off views. It was, as I've said, May. The honeysucklish white flowers that erupt from the bases of the leaves had already made their appearance, been pollinated, withered off. Now up and down the tree's limbs grew clusters of green knobs, hard knuckles of fruit known as drupes or, more commonly, cherries. Inside each cherry lay two seeds, their flat sides facing one another, their integrity protected by a silver mucilage. The tree was at least five years old; that's how long it takes for *Coffea arabica* to yield its fruit. It would produce some two thousand coffee cherries that year, or some four thousand seeds, and however many cups of coffee. Even its shiny, droopy, dark green leaves were, I knew, laced with caffeine, but standing there beside Nora's prized birds of paradise, it was more symbol than source, more statement than utility. A coffee farm is massed with trees—some four hundred to one thousand per acre. A single tree set off in a well of light stands as a reminder, a signifier, of coffee's extraordinary journey across centuries and seas.

Western mythology suggests that coffee was discovered by an Ethiopian goatherd named Kaldi. There were the goats, say the legend, getting all kicky and giddy in their tropical forest, and there was the befuddled Kaldi, trying to discern the source of their joy. When he noticed the goats nibbling the cherries off a woody shrub, he thought he had better try one for himself. He did, not much liking the taste, it seems, but enjoying the high he apparently got while turning the drupe over in his mouth. Kaldi chose to share his discovery with an abbot, who, according to the legend, quickly decided that the stimulating fruit was a gift from God, a provocateur that would keep his monks awake for the prayers they had to say all night.

First eaten as fresh fruit, then crushed into balls of animal fat and chomped on by nomadic warriors as some of the world's first power bars, coffee wasn't prepared as a hot drink until one thousand or so years ago. It wasn't prepared in its modern form until the 1400s, when metal pots were created and water could be boiled. By the mid-sixteenth century, coffee was so powerfully popular that proprietors in Constantinople, Cairo, and Mecca were opening the world's first coffeehouses. And the more popular coffee got, the more the Arabs who had been cultivating it began to guard its secrets, forbidding foreigners from taking germinating beans home.

Smugglers, of course, succeeded, and soon coffee was being cultivated and brewed the world over, coffeehouses had become regular meeting places, and Europeans were devising schemes to exploit the product. But it would thrive as a crop only in environments that resembled the ones whence it had come—lands of sunshine and moderate rainfall, lands where the temperature averaged some seventy degrees and where the flora was never under the threat of frost, lands where the soils were rich and renewable, where there was the appropriate range of altitudes. Lacking in mineral wealth, challenged by a proliferation of volcanic hills (where soil erosion negates the viability of many annual crops), out of time with cocoa, balsam, indigo, El Salvador, in the nineteenth century, found its match with coffee. For better and for worse, it found its future.

This one tree cordoned off like sculpture in Nora's immaculate garden had defined a nation's modern times: El Salvador's prosperity and poverty and politics, its murders, reprisals, and grace all had tracers back to coffee. It had defined my husband's family, too, and it had shaped my husband's soul. Who he was, what he thought, how he remembered, how he dreamed, what he wanted, what he feared, what he was lonely for, why he kept the secrets he kept was all tangled up—sometimes distinctly, sometimes vaguely—with coffee. A crop I'd never seen before. A drink I am not fond of. I stopped taking photographs and squinted up at the scrap of sky that I could see from where I was standing. I'd be flying home in a couple of days. I'd ask Bill for explanations. I would hope he'd find the words.

Sisters

ART

⚬⚬⚬

I met the man I would marry in the summer of 1983. He was the artist. I was the woman who wrote down what she saw. I was the child of privilege, the daughter of two parents who had prepared their three kids well for the Ivy League and its equivalents, and I had traveled—Europe, Canada, the American West—traveled with my comforts, traveled with a camera that sanctioned my idea of beauty. This man I met who would become my husband had stories to tell, and I would prompt them and listen, pretend that I was brave enough and sufficiently capacious for all that he remembered.

Two years later I stood in an ivory dress behind an ivory veil and found this man down the distance of an aisle. He was what my idea of beauty had become—slender and eloquent in his posture and his stride, tempestuous about the eyes, tender in the way he used his hands, in the way he knew to touch me—and also, he was startling in the tuxedo he had borrowed, the hair he had had cut for the occasion. *I am here,* he'd called me two hours before, from the office of the Presbyterian minister. *I am here.* As if I thought that perhaps he wouldn't be. As if I was afraid, and of course I was afraid, that the countries that would always lie between us would always, and finally, lie between us. *I am here.* That's what he said before we married.

In the church that day there were Nora, Adela, Ana Ruth, Martha, elaborate and surreal as tropical birds in their yellow, azure, coffee-cherry colored linens. In the church there were Bill's brothers and my family, my parents, our friends, the minister, the organist, the sound of June rain against the roof, the sprays of flowers, white flowers, were they orchids, or were they roses that I'm remembering now as lilies?

And in the back of the church, in the final pew, alone, was Mario, Bill's father, a man I had not met until two nights before. I watched him as I waited for the right music to begin. I watched and I wondered about what had brought him there alone, about all that had precipitated the separation, then the divorce, now this chasm in a church. Mario had come from another country, not Nora's own. He had grown up with English, not with Spanish. He could not roll the r's and he had not loved the farm, and he had not learned to love it, couldn't gentle a tenderling into a tree. And maybe he could not imagine the land when it was cattle instead of trees, when it was Maya instead of Pipil, when it was sea instead of soil, when it was nothing. And maybe he hadn't clawed his fingers into the earth and pulled himself up, and then up again into the company of the dead and the turkey sentries. Perhaps Mario had never tried, or wouldn't try, or had not tried faithfully enough, or perhaps he'd tried with all his soul, and it had felt like thieving, finally.

"Cleaving" is a perverted word. It means to separate and sever. It means to stick fast and adhere. It means to divide and then cohere and then hold fast. It means to challenge the woman in the ivory gown. It means to challenge the man dressed in black. It means to challenge them both as they stand and wait for the processional on the occasion of their wedding.

In the early years of our marriage, Bill and I shared a studio. We lived in a walk-up apartment then, on the fringe middle of Philadelphia, and we gave the front room over to our art, the back room over to our sleep; in the crowded, crooked middle room we ate our uninspired meals. Bill stayed up late to work. I slept, but woke up early. We passed each other in the dark in the awkward kitchen, Bill leaving the studio light on for me, I leaving the bed covers warm.

In the fog after sleep, when I had no relationship yet with language, I'd sit on the floor where Bill had been sitting and watch the watercolors drying on his paintings, his light pencil tracings sipped away by the coagulating colors. The work felt alive, more whole than words could ever be, and in the hazy fume of awakening I believed that if I stared at the paintings hard enough I'd see the soul and the center of my husband. Weren't watercolors windows? Didn't they suggest the unmediated, the true? Peering down into the paintings Bill had made while I was sleeping, I found the tremors of the stories that he had not told to me, the parts of himself that he couldn't quite explain, or had chosen not to, or was still working out the meaning of. The paintings were Bill's; he didn't want to try to sell them.

But the paintings were also mine, I thought, because I fiercely loved them. If Bill was quiet with me, restrained in Philadelphia, at least I had, on the floor of our apartment, evidence of all I'd always suspected him to be. The paintings existed because Don Alberto had understood that his grandson was an artist, that his talent must be succored. He paid for the art lessons, Bill told me. Invited Bill to live at his house whenever Bill needed the privacy to paint. Bill never sought or hoped for

praise, never looked for validation; never have I known him to
need a compliment. He has only ever wanted time with the art
that keeps his memories whole, and this is what marriage
teaches me to give. It's love that tethers Bill to this place that's
not his home. Love that has left him with his losses, speaking the
language that does not sound like him. It is important, I think,
not to press too hard. Important to give him sanctuary.

Though inevitably I ask questions, hem the paintings in
with words. Back then I asked more than might have been,
strictly speaking, fair—waiting for dinner to inquire about the
woman with Yoko Ono hair and the catastrophic face whom I'd
seen drying on the paper. Her name, I'd learn, was Siguanaba;
she was a witch. The odd dog? That was the black dog, *cadejo
negro*. The little boy with the gigantic hat was the mischievous,
elfin Cipitio, and the oxcarts rattling down the road without
their oxen were for announcing to the living that they were
about to enter the land of the dead. These paintings, then, held
the other stories of the farm, the ones the maids told to keep the
kids from running too far down the hill.

Siguanaba frightened me most; Bill was brutal with her ren-
dering. On the first morning, she'd appear fluid and sinister on
the buckled Canson paper, her black hair wild and coarse and
hanging nearly to her knees. Only a slip of face would show
through all that hair—a longitudinal section of ghastly forehead,
nose, and chin—and below the face, there was the naked pale-
ness between her breasts, the triangle of hair above her legs:
hoary, wet, unsettled. But the next day, the same Siguanaba
would appear on the same, more buckled paper, her hair now
closed in across her breasts and more like rampant, grizzled fur.
Her face would be colluded, skull-like, hollow. A hiss of green
paint would escape the fraction of her lips. Subsequently, the
next day, her fur would be more than fur; it would glow with an

odd green iridescence, have feather hatch marks all around. And then a hand would break through the mass of feathered fur, a fantastic claw with fantastic talons, each with an aggressive animal thickness.

Only the doomed have ever seen Siguanaba. She lives in gorges between low rocks and wind, her black hair in intractable wind knots, her skin sometimes transparent on her hands and sometimes furred. Her feet attach at the wrong angles to her legs, in such a way that her toes point assward and those who see her coming don't understand, at first, that she's coming straight for them. Venture too far, to the river, let's say, and you will feel her growl in your ear, her hot smarmy breath on your neck. Afterwards? It isn't clear. Those who've lived to tell the tale are as good as lunatics. Those who have even barely got the whiff of her have stumbled home that very evening with a fever. Or so Bill said, when I asked him.

Bill's *cadejo negro* was also—is still—a conundrum. A doggy-looking dog in places, except for the eyes, which are more than bloodshot red, and the horns, which might belong to a ram, except that they're arching in the wrong direction; Bill admits to having construed these for art's sake. It's a black dog. It's got goat's feet. It has a white-dog brother who is kind, but he—the black dog—is comprehensively evil. You don't know this at first. You trust the *cadejo negro*, you let him travel with you, you tell him pieces of your life. You rest under the shade of a tree, and he rests beside you. You give the dog a name, you think that you will bring him home. But the black dog wants to involve you in his crimes. He wants you to steal for him, or kill, and he's greedy. He doesn't let up once he's involved you in his devilish plans, and the only cure for him is garlic, rubbed over every pore of your skin. It offends the dog, your fetid garlicness, and he finally begs off, goes trotting up the road after new victims. Again, you meet up with the dog, you get a fever. You come home hot, and your family knows what happened.

And you get a fever, too, if you cross paths with Cipitio, the little ash-eating urchin whose mother's bad mothering left him a perpetual seven-year-old. And you get a fever, but it doesn't much matter, if the oxcarts start rattling for you at night. You might as well give in to your own death, they say. The oxcarts know when it's time to go, and there's no use fighting the clamoring spirits.

After my first trip to El Salvador, I'd look for signs of witches, devils, spirits in the photographs that I'd brought home, for evidence of Siguanaba or an oxcart rattle. I'd look for some correspondence between my husband's art and my own. I'd look for missing things and found things, piecing the images together, like poems. My photos spread out on the floor at an angle to Bill's paintings, under the brazen lamp we shared, in the silence of the hour before dawn, I looking for what I hadn't been able to see when I was there, for whatever nerves had blocked out, or impatience. I'd study the photos as if a stranger had snapped them, because it seemed, in so many ways, that a stranger had—the images alerting me to things I hadn't thought I'd seen, to details I'd not dialed into, to arrangements of color and light I'd failed at first to appreciate. To two children, for example, whose path I'd followed down a steep gulley on a second day up at the farm. I'd kneeled in the dust to take their picture, and they'd turned to look straight back at me, posing for nothing, waiting, the boy with his hands thrown down to his sides, the girl nibbling a leaf from a nearby tree. On the farm I'd thought of them as children—he might have been four, she might have been seven—but afterwards, studying the photograph, it was their seriousness that struck me, the way she had taken care to tuck her polka-dotted blouse into the pale muddy slip that was her skirt, the way he stood there unashamed of his too-snug shirt, his sagging gym shorts. Their legs were stockinged in dust, and every limb on them was skinny, and they didn't try to speak to me, they just waited for the camera to click off.

Another photograph, two sisters this time, sharing a patch of shade on the side of their one-room house. I'd stolen the picture like a secret, snuck up from the opposite side of the makeshift porch and shot it through the shadows, so that the vegetation in the distance had bleached yellow and the kids themselves stood out in stark relief to both the dark patches and the sun. The older sister looked away. The little one looked curious, looked as if she might decide to come to me and reveal whatever she had crumpled in the tight fist of her left hand. I was aware that day on the farm of how the family had stacked its firewood so neatly in a squarish mound, aware of the jugs and milk cartons and pots that hung like notes on sheet music from the ceiling, aware of the man's shirt and woman's dress that had been thrown out over a rope to dry. But in Philadelphia it was the little girl I studied, the one who seemed to want to come near. To lift her naked foot and arrive at where I'd stood with my camera, trespassing.

And what about the photographs, just two, that I'd taken at the water hole that Bill had described that first day, when we sat up in the tree. *In the morning, before anyone else was awake, we'd race down the hill in our pajamas and dive into the old water hole.* We'd hiked all the way down the mountain to find it—Bill and his brother Rodi and his best childhood friend, Rafael, along with one of the farm's administrators who'd macheted tall grasses to the side for my less surefooted sake—and when we'd gotten there Bill, Rodi, and Rafael had stripped off their shirts and yahoo'ed like kids and slid down a muddy slope into the natural, coffee-colored pool. The first photograph shows only the troop I'd traveled with—Rodi already doused and standing waist high in the waters, Bill mid-slide with his arms upraised, the administrator in his peacock-blue nylon shirt, flicking off cigarette ashes as he watched. The second photo, taken at a different, wider angle, shows Bill, Rodi, Rafael arm over arm and soaking wet, water waists high, in the stone-and-tall-grass–encircled pool. But it's what happens on the margins of that photograph that caught my eye in Philadelphia, the four utterly naked peasant boys who sit on the pool's rocky ledge, their hands in their chins. They are watching not the men but the woman with the camera, the one planted on the edge of things behind the barricade of her lens. I didn't remember that they'd been there until I'd gotten home, to Philadelphia. Until I was sitting there studying my husband's paintings of things that don't exist.

For many years I tried to move beyond my own prejudices, boundaries, fears, tried to enter my husband's territory—hoping for more than he naturally thought to give me, asking questions when I could stand his silence no more. I would ask, and I would read, and I would study the paintings he left not for me but for himself in the morning—the dead Archbishop Romero with the red X across his heart, the Cipitio swallowed by a gargantuan straw hat, the Siguanaba who would return, angrier and uglier than the last time. I would take what I knew of Tiburcio's life and turn it into a story—write of him making love to Nicha by the river, beyond the bend where the women were washing; write of him fitting his hand to his machete and watching his son's tormentor fall, miraculously, into the blade. I would study the wispy photographs of Don Alberto as an old man, ask Bill to remember what he could of his own generation's civil war and mass reprisals, ask him to tell me how it was that his mother, after a father's death, after a war, after a divorce, after her leg had been shattered in a fall, after her three sons had gone from

home, Bill leading the way, had managed to keep coffee growing up and down those sacred hills.

When Bill woke in those years speaking Spanish, I would
try to understand what he had said. But he would only want me
to hold him then, only say that he'd wakened too soon from a
dream.

Ripened coffee cherries

LUCK

———⧓———

$\mathcal{B}$y 1970, there were six farms in Don Alberto's care, one each to be left to his five children, one to be transferred, at his death, to his delicate wife, Tere, who would surprise herself and all who knew her by outliving her husband for twenty years. The farms were named for what they were; each had, in its way, a personality. There was Buena Vista, Good View, the little nest of coffee land that would go to Martha, who'd married an Italian and moved to Rome. There was Adela's fecund San Joaquín, which they preferred to call Los Amates, after the trees that grew in those hills. *You should see the trees, Beth, huge and beautiful. Full of worms in winter, full of birds, so many birds, all year-round, and reproducing two ways: by pods, by seeds.*

There was La Cruces, The Cross, for Beto, Don Alberto's only son; there was Santa Teresa de los Ranchos, for Tere; and San Antonio, or St. Anthony's, was, of course, the farm picked out and planted and nurtured for Bill's ever-pragmatic mother, Nora. Finally, there was La Suerte, or Luck, which was to be left to Ana Ruth, the second eldest, who loved to dance but who had never had much luck. A gorgeous farm, La Suerte was only pastures when Don Alberto bought it in the 1940s, only coffee by the time he was through, save for a swath of low emerald-colored grass where he let his horses run.

But it was Luck, as it turns out, that almost did in Don Alberto, and almost extinguished my husband at the same time. Again it is a jeep that conveys us to the story, and, again, the mountainous, murderous farm road. Don Alberto is at the wheel, and Bill's youngest brother, Rodi, is in the passenger's seat, and Bill, just careening into adolescence, is in the back behind Rodi, with his best friend, Rafael, at his side. The boys are going riding. They are aiming to take the horses out for exercise, while Don Alberto, who was seventy-five now, his thick hair a mantle of absolute white, pays the workers on the farm. "What happened," Bill says, "what happened is this: We went driving up one of those steep dirt mountain inclines, we went driving down one, we went up another. And then we hit the mountain peak and started going down again. You know those roads, Beth. You know how it is; you've seen it—all precipice and air on one side, a fat wall of rocks on the other, but this, this was some stretch of road. And it was then—when we started down the longest and steepest and most treacherous part—that my grandfather started waving his arms, started saying something, shouting, but we couldn't hear him. It was a jeep. You can't hear a damned thing in a jeep on a farm road. Rafael and I—we had no idea what he was saying."

Or what he wanted.

And so the jeep kept hurtling down the much-too-steep dirt road, the unguarded precipice on the one side, the relentless wall of rocks on the other. *Oh shit,* Bill remembers thinking, as the machine kept accelerating, *he's going fast; he's going really fast.* And still Don Alberto's arm was waving, still he was shouting, but still none but Don Alberto knew that the brake was shot and the jeep was wild and the four of them were about to crash. There are no outs on roads like that. You either fly over the mountain ridge and keep on flying, or you smash like a physicist's atoms into the rocks.

"I turned around," Bill says. "Instinct. I grabbed the back of the seat, I don't know why, except that there were no seat belts, there was nothing to strap me in. It's what I thought to do." He could have hurled head-first through the windshield. Out through glass, and into stone, all smithereens. Don Alberto was careening the jeep into the wall of rocks. Steering fiercely and blinklessly that way, because the other way was down and over, big riffles of air, and out. When they hit, *son of a bitch,* at whatever speed they hit, it was like the end of the world. Rodi was an instant crumple on the floor; Bill was an ass-forwards throb against Rodi's seat; Rafael's legs were torqued and partly skinless. Don Alberto, for his part, was left holding the snapped-off steering wheel, rivers of blood pouring backwards from his fingers down his arms. Afterwards, Bill lay there on his back, studying the sky, confused: Was this life or death? All that dust, he says, pouring down, slow motion, and then the spare tire that had been thrown off at impact started falling back down to earth, like some giant rubber bomb. Falling and falling, until it smacked up against the hood of the car and bounced away again. "I watched it fall. It felt like hours. I thought I'd broken my back, but Rafael said that if I had, I'd have been crying, and I wasn't; none of us were. We were in shock. We were okay. We were alive." Bill is here now, with me. He is our child's father because Don Alberto chose the rocks over the air.

One minute later, Bill says, one single minute, he's certain of this though his sense of time was skewed, an overloaded pickup truck turned the corner and came in a racket and a hurry up that dusty road. "We'd have gone smack into it and died for sure," Bill says, "if my grandfather hadn't had the guts to crash.

Can you imagine that? At his age? Having the guts to throw a jeep into the rocks?"

But it scared him, Bill says. It scared Don Alberto because this time he hadn't just narrowly missed his own death, he'd almost lost three kids, three very young men he considered friends, who hadn't yet had their lives to live. Shortly after the accident, he sold La Suerte: couldn't bear the sight of that stretch of road, couldn't bear remembering what might have happened. The horses, the emerald patch, the coffee: all of Luck was sold, thrust into another farmer's hands. Ana Ruth was willed the money from the sale, and Don Alberto never drove that road again.

In 1939, the Asociación Cafetalera de El Salvador hauled its finest coffee to the Golden Gate International Exposition in California and sang its praises to the world with a chirpy pamphlet:

> As you enjoy the flavor of a delicious cup of coffee, has it ever occurred to you what efforts and methods are employed in the tropics by growers of coffee to furnish the world with this wonderful product of nature . . . "The Golden Bean"? This is the bean from which you brew that cheering and invigorating drink which cheers you when you feel depressed, and when you are gay and happy, stimulates without harm.
>
> Perhaps you have heard of the little Republic of El Salvador, whence comes the finest, the most wholesome, the most palatable, and the most aromatic of all coffees, which is of such a high quality that it is used as a blend to improve the grade and

flavor of other coffees so as to make them more marketable . . . .

El Salvador is an entirely peaceful country. Its inhabitants are hard-working and peace-loving. There is no unemployment in El Salvador; on the contrary, there are times when there is a marked scarcity of workers. The population as a whole consists of a mixture of Spaniards and natives.

El Salvador may be reached from San Francisco by water in seven days, and by airplane in three days. Soon this trip may be made by automobile over the Pan-American highway, now under construction . . . .

The Story of El Salvador Coffee, the pamphlet is called, a tiny, brightly covered thing, presenting winking sepia-tinted photos within. There is a picture of a man wearing a Panama hat and a gun in his holster, directing the transplanting of tenderlings at his plantation. There is a snapshot of a pig-tailed lass gleefully serving a basketful of cherries to the camera. There are photographs of the *beneficios* and the *patios de café,* where the coffee cherries are transformed into product, and there is a full-page image of a woman thrusting her hands into a tree. "Native women carefully pick the ripe coffee cherries by hand," the caption says.

The pamphlet is charming in its effect. A utopia here on earth. An ideal. And also: a calculated marketing campaign for a country at the end of a devastating decade, a country in the confusing thick of reconstruction, in a world still stumbling about at the end of a depression. This was the late 1930s, after all. The rock-bottom coffee prices, the *matanza,* the countrywide paralysis were not yet distant memories. All across El Salvador, coffee *fincas* had gone bankrupt, coffee cherries had rotted in trees, land had been repossessed by banks. The future was in the hands of Maximiliano Hernández Martínez, the dictator they called El Brujo, who had engineered the massacre of some thirty thousand Indians seven years before.

Martínez was a strange man: bloodthirsty but also obsessed with the occult; trained in the law and in military tactics, but perpetually seduced by sorcery. To the outbreak of a smallpox epidemic, he responded by demanding that all street lamps be covered with red cellophane, so as to cleanse the air, he said, and arrest the disease. To help the children of his country "better receive the beneficial emanations of the planet," he insisted that they toss away their shoes and travel barefoot. El Brujo valued the lives of insects and animals over humans (for they, unlike people, have but one life), conducted seances in his home, fell in love with the notion of fascism, and kept the specter of communism at bay with reminders of the massacre he'd propagated.

And yet he'd done his country some good—declaring a moratorium on debts, opening doors to agricultural credit, founding the Mejoramiento Social to improve the living standard of the poor. He curbed the crime rate through fear alone. He promoted the construction of the Pan-American Highway. And, in a somewhat perverse if apparently well-meant measure designed to protect the economic interests of the campesinos, he prohibited the use of the powered machinery then coming into vogue for the manufacture of shoes and sisal sacks. Little by little, in other words, El Brujo returned the economy to the coffee growers. He pointed to the red cherry as the cure.

Those who saw opportunity where others saw defeated land, those who wanted rule over their own lives, those who wanted to tie their fortunes to the serendipity of coffee cherries needed a modicum of capital and plenty of patience to see them through. Don Alberto, it seems, had both. He also had dreams and faith, and in 1940, working as a land assessment officer at the Banco Salvadoreño, he found the parcel of earth that would become the heart of St. Anthony's Farm. It wasn't coffee land. It was *potrero*, cattle pasture—land that had left its owners broke and defaulting on their Banco loans. Taking out a loan of his own, Don Alberto promised to make the land grow beans, promised the first yield's profits to the bank. Nora was eight and dark-haired, pretty and petite, already settled in with her cache of lifelong best friends, when her father came home a *finca* owner, her future in his land. She remembers, she says, the day trips the family began to take from their modest home in Santa Tecla up the pocked dirt road toward El Limón. She remembers the cattle that somehow clung to the intensely angled earth and gathered beneath the shade of ancient trees. She remembers her father planting the tenderlings deep in the soil. Later, Adela writes, when the tenderlings had grown into trees, when the limbs grew fertile with cherries, when the first profits had been delivered to the bank, Nora, Ana Ruth, Martha, Beto, Adela, Tere, and Alberto would go and spend three months at St. Anthony's, helping the campesinos pick coffee. *My father bought us small baskets so that we could pick too, and Tito, who is Nora's fore-man now, was just a little kid then, like us. He and his brothers and the other kids from the farm would come at night to play the games that my father and mother taught us. Oh, it was really great, and oh, I could go on and on, but, Beth, I will never finish.*

For all it had been through, El Salvador still had its charms. The early nightfalls, the stunning daybreaks, the music of so many birds yet in the trees. And coming up and down the dirt roads, from the hills into the city and back up into the hills, came the farmer with his fruit- and vegetable-laden oxcart, and also the milkman, who would strap four large cans of milk over his horse's rump. *The milkmen would come into town with their milk,*

Beth, and they would whistle at the doors of their customers. The maid would bring a pitcher from the kitchen; the milkman would ladle out his milk. And when his cans were empty the milkman would go and buy his corn at the market in town, filling the empty milk cans with the corn. He'd add water to the corn, and he'd take his horse back up the roads, and by the time he was home in the hills, the corn and water had cleaned his cans. It was a beautiful thing to see, and to hear—the sound of the milk sloshing in the cans, the cans rattling against the cans on the rump of the horse, that whistle. Even then we knew that it was a beautiful thing.

Converting cattle pastures into a coffee plantation requires mind and heart and time, and beyond all else, respect for hills, weather, sky, the temper and temperament of soil. Set down upon the so-called Belt of Fire, El Salvador is, as has been said, volcanic, moody, in ever-fickle flux. It changes personality on a whim. "Where lovely valleys extended some centuries ago offering luxuriant vegetation, now towering volcanoes intercept the horizon," wrote one historian in 1956. "Where brooks rippled and sang merrily on their way through quiet fields, now roaring rivers cascade down high cliffs into deep canyons on their way to sea. Where formerly lush green vegetation soothed the sight, now great black lava fields extend for miles. Where formerly placid pools and lakes contributed water to vegetation, now deep fissures mark the same spots and dry fields surround the area where a seismic upheaval drank the precious liquid in thirsty gulps, leaving a barren soil."

El Salvador, the land itself, is alive. It contains the secrets of its many incarnations—not just those thrust upon it by its own combustible heat and fire, but those seeded and sprung by human hands. Across the face of El Salvador, an aggressive agricultural history is writ large—in the denuded countryside, in the depleted soils, in the endlessly diverted waterways. Time and again, Salvadorans have asked for more from their tiny swatch of land, and the land has either adapted or rebelled.

Within every crop there lies a story. The vaunted godlike maize, the country's first true crop, was born of fire. The Indians set forests ablaze to make room for their fields. They burned down corn stubble at the end of each dry season to accommodate a new sweep of seeds. Fire agriculture was a pre-Columbian invention, and the tradition was continued for centuries; El Salvadoran topography, vistas, attitudes today all reflect this philosophy of flames. Burning things down so as to grow things up, destroying so as to create, Salvadorans brought dust storms and erosion to their country; they scattered the rare, glorious birds that hid in trees. They fed a fledgling nation without plow, wheel, or draft animal, and that, for the time being, was the point.

Cocoa left its legacy as well. Grown on trees that take five years, at least, to mature, cocoa makes for a pretty crop and a delicate environmental proposition. The cocoa orchards that spread across certain slopes of El Salvador in the sixteenth century fueled the economy both as coinage and as crop. Every cocoa tree was born of rituals—the seeds were blessed under a full moon and aromatic herbs; at the conclusion of the planting and sowing cycle, the planters went home to their wives and made passionate love. Between each seedling was planted a *madre cacao*, a big-leafed tree whose canopy protected the crop from excessive sun and rain and whose poisonous roots kept harmful insects at bay. Cocoa trees need water year-round; El Salvador's climate does not provide it. So here again, the earth was made unlike itself, as channels were cut into the rocks and soils and streams diverted from their native orientations. To keep a cocoa orchard yielding, old trees must be tirelessly yanked out, weeds must be kept at bay, weather itself must cooperate. The Indians, it seems, were graceful cocoa growers. Until usurious Spanish labor practices and the spread of Spanish diseases killed off a large percentage of the native population, until a volcanic eruption swiped an entire bank of orchards off one mountainside and the Venezuelans took the lead as cocoa growers, there was, in El Salvador, an expanse of cocoa trees, some orchards estimated at fifteen thousand trees strong. Macaws nested in the canopies. Wildlife took refuge.

But indigo followed cocoa, and again the land was plundered. Shrublike and ugly, native to both the Old World and the New, indigo yielded derivatives—the bluish dye and medicinal properties of its leaves—that had been exploited in Europe since the time of the Roman Empire. Before the Spanish conquest, Indians had collected the occasional leaf as it was needed from wild plants. But after the Spanish came to town, indigo was elevated in stature; the Spanish sought indigo wealth, indigo prestige. Devoting large banks of land to the weedlike plant, force-employing Indians in its cultivation and processing, the bullish Spanish set old-growth and secondary forests aflame, burned down the scrub. Fires raged across the landscape; travelers described the eeriness of passing through.

Most effectively grown on well-drained and fertile soils, indigo was sown across the lower slopes and valleys of the central highlands; it dominated what would later become Santa Tecla. Land was cleared from January to March. Seeds were scattered by hand. Cattle were encouraged to trample the soil and pack down the seeds. The April rains fed the seeds; the plants erupted from the earth; the cows, chowing freely through communal Indian vegetable gardens, left the bad-tasting indigo alone. September and October brought the indigo harvest, with the Indians collecting only the leaves of the two- to three-year-old plants, where the dye concentrations were greatest. After their third year of growing, the depleted six-foot shrubs were axed and burnt away, and the fields were reseeded, or left fallow.

The processing of indigo went on in the central mills of each estate, with each mill sited near a source of running water and encircled by the huts of Indian workers. "The mill consisted of two large stone basins," the historian David Browning tells us. "After the indigo had been cut, it was steeped in water in the first basin, weighted down by lengths of timber, and left for twenty-four hours. At the appropriate time a *puntero* drained off the liquid into a deeper basin that was equipped with a wheel powered by horses, oxen or water, and beaten until a yellowish foam formed. The remaining liquid was drained away, the foam removed, placed into large linen bags to strain off further liquid, and finally formed into blocks that were sundried and packed into loads, *zurrones,* each of 214 pounds."

And all this was done by a native population that had to be coerced to work the mills. Indigo workers died in legendary numbers: it was hard work; living conditions were poor; the Spanish bosses offered little sympathy and sometimes beat their people bloody; and beyond all that, infectious diseases struck the workers down, as flies congregated in the rotting waste. Fever-stricken, despondent, overwhelmed, many of the enslaved natives attempted to shortcut their misery by taking their own lives. They would sleep in the fields and offer their bodies to voracious, deadly insects. They'd swallow poisonous herbs or hang themselves from trees. Dispirited and seeing no way out, the Indian population was further effaced during the indigo years, meaning that it wasn't just the land that was laid victim to a crop; it was a people.

Indigo, in due time, ran its course—competition from other indigo-growing countries and, in the nineteenth century, from synthetic dies, depleted its actual and imagined use. A new crop was needed to sustain El Salvador, and this time the government systematically sought alternatives—vanilla, sarsaparilla, tobacco, timber, hides, gums, resins, fruits, herbs, agave. In 1838, a gold medal was offered to the first farmer who could harvest silk. In 1855, another promise was publicized: the first farmer who could have one thousand grape vines ready for harvest would prosper mightily. But little stuck. "When a substitute for indigo was being sought in the nineteenth century, and the government distributed free young plants of a number of commercial crops, only coffee prospered," relates the historian Alastair White. "It is of course possible that for some plants the wrong varieties were tried, and that El Salvador could successfully grow grapes, for instance, or citrus fruit. At any rate, the climate has proved unsuitable for the varieties so far introduced."

And so came coffee—quietly introduced to the country in the early 1800s, planted and harvested by the Brazilian schoolteacher in 1839, upheld as an antidote to the demise of indigo, and yet another reason to set the country alight with flames, to bombard the population with the sound of axed-down forests. By 1848, local observers were expressing concern about the rapid deforestation demanded by the crop, opining, at one point, that "the custom is for workmen with axes to fell trees in order to clean ground for coffee plantings, with no thought for preserving the more useful and valuable timber." In the 1850s, one visitor to the country found himself bewildered, surrounded, as he was, "by fires on all sides."

But coffee—the same conclusion gets drawn again and again—was right for El Salvador, where the hilly terrain is not predisposed to row crops, and where every square inch of land must be made to matter. El Salvador's well-drained, fertile soils were right, its climate was right, its rainfall was just right for coffee. With success came more proposals, more promises: any person planting more than five thousand bushes of coffee would be exempt from municipal taxes for the next ten years; any person working coffee would be exempt from military draft; any coffee produced during a certain seven years would escape the export tax. By the 1870s, the messy mix of communal lands and private estates was raising eyebrows, raising concerns. By the 1880s, native villages were disintegrating as members left the homestead to work the farms up in the hills.

Forests, shrubs were axed to the ground. Coffee overtook indigo. There were small plots, there were large plots, the rich and the not-so-rich were growing trees. Soon coffee was virtually El Salvador's only export crop. Soon huge tracts of once-communal land was placed in the hands of private owners. Roads were built east–west and north–south, ports and ships were fortified to help expedite crop production and trade. Santa Ana, Sonsonate, Ahuachapán, San Salvador, and Santa Tecla were systematically remade with coffee trees.

$\mathscr{B}$y 1940, when Don Alberto spent 28,000 colones for the cattle pastures that would become the heart of St. Anthony's Farm, the planting and nurturing of coffee had become its own exquisite form of art. The highest yields, it was understood, would be achieved through a mix of things—through the right ratio of shade trees to coffee plants, through the calculated replacement of older trees, through the careful conservation and manuring of the soil, through the establishment of a trusted labor force.

To turn a pasture into a coffee farm, one begins by compensating for so much steepness and carving terraces into the earth. One might bank these walls with rock or one might choose to plant the long-rooted izote and cactus instead; either

way, one must give the young trees their footing. When the terraces are ready and erosion fended off, one collects the coffee
seedlings that have been grown on nursery beds. Into the ter-
raced earth, these tenderlings are set, and among the tenderlings
are planted shade trees—*madre cacao, pepeto,* other hardwoods.
While the tenderlings grow, one weeds, one prunes, one plants
some more. In three to five years' time, the coffee trees will bear
their fruit.

There is, finally, the picking to take care of, November
through January of every year, each tree picked two or three
times as the cherries turn their waxy red. As soon as the cherries are off the trees and any stray green fruits are separated from
the red, they are taken to a *beneficio,* and washed for hours in
warm water, where they are induced to ferment and split, to
yield their fine twin beans. Freed of their fruit, the beans are
taken into the sun and dried. A milling operation strips the
parchment husk from every bean, and then the beans are graded
and bundled for export according to brand standards.

Plantation coffee growing is for those who can look into
the future and believe. It is for those who understand the enor-
mity of the investment: in trees that must be pruned and regu-
larly uprooted, in workers who must be cared for, learned from,
trusted. For most, and certainly for Don Alberto, building a coffee *finca* means taking out a loan, and it means working hard for
many years without a yield. It means putting oneself at the
mercy of weather, international prices, uncertainty, interest rates,
the natural human fates that will befall the families that help
trees grow.

When Don Alberto bought the cattle pasture that became
St. Anthony's Farm, El Salvador's love affair with coffee had
been sorely tested for a decade—by a depression, by a massacre,
by the sight of so many coffee *fincas* left to rot upon the hills.

Despite the cheery claims of hopeful pamphlets, new investments in coffee land were still seen by many as speculation of the rankest sort.

But land prices were low and opportunity had come calling and Don Alberto was not looking back, he was looking ahead. He was not turning away from the dream he'd fashioned while waiting out his house arrest in La Libertad. Soon enough, the land he trusted, planted, cared for would bring him his hoped-for luck: the soil was fertile, the tenderlings prospered, World War II and then the Korean War would send coffee prices soaring. Soon enough, Don Alberto would take the profits from his yield and toss the colones to the wind in that tree-limned park of Santa Tecla. With the passing of the years, he would quietly, steadily extend and diversify his holdings; he would leave his job at the bank and settle completely into the coffee life. He would buy a plantation for each of his children and a pretty little *finca* for his wife, and he would love nothing more devotedly than the honeysuckle smell of coffee blossoms on the breeze.

San Joaquín

FREEDOM

—⟨∞⟩—

 $\mathcal{T}$ here are, as it turns out, three photographs of Don Alberto dating from the years he spent in jail. They arrive in winter, when I am stewing with a fever. When I open Adela's envelope I'm sure, at first, that I am looking at old black-and-whites of my own husband. I know that face, I think. I know those heavy eyebrows and that broad nose and the set of that jaw and the kept secrets of those lips. I know the way that slender body strikes its balance in that chair, the way the jacket is thrown open to the air, the way the right hand lies loose across the right thigh, the way the left hand is more assertive, more alive. I know the eyes that can stare forever without blinking, the honest eyes, incapable of fear. The man of the photographs twice poses in a cobbled courtyard, once stands in the narrow plaster corridor of the jailhouse proper; three times he is the foreground before a background of companionable men. In the courtyard shots, he is dressed in formal wear—white, neat, pressed slacks, white heel-high boots, a thin, diagonally striped tie much like the tie that my husband would wear when we first married, a jacket that is dark as black in the two-toned photograph. *These are the pictures I have been promising,* I read Adela's note now, several times. *This is my father when he was in jail.*

It is inconceivable. The photos are not in the least how I'd imagined them, not as I was certain they would be. I'd expected the delimitations of steel bars. The traditional tunics of the accused. A pleading look about the eyes. Defeat dampening the shoulders. At the very least: impatience. But the man I meet in these startling photographs is unhurried and impeccable, unrepentant for his part in the failed coup. He has, according to all available evidence, made new friends while he remains in jail waiting to go free or to die.

No one knows how the jail term affected Don Alberto. He didn't speak of it, Adela writes. It's not what we talked about, Bill says. There is nothing in the record to suggest that he grew kinder or more thoughtful, or that he hardened or grew bitter, or that what he thought of love was altered, or that his politics twisted and softened or faded to irrelevance, except that he posed for those photographs, and he saved them; he kept proof of his incarceration for himself. The past, as always, is veiled, suspicious, cunning.

I make do with my fallible imagination. I make his heart, because of a commuted sentence, even larger than it genetically was. I take him up into the hills above El Limón in 1940 with an outsized kindness and a generous predisposition toward those who had endured hardships that would always be far more harrowing than his own. This is hagiography, perhaps, but it's not without its moorings. There are stories. There are photographs. There is the fondness that survived a civil war. There is the legacy, for to this day Don Alberto is remembered well by the campesinos of his farms. By the old ones. By the second generations, and by the third, who know him only through the tales they've been told, and only through the fact of his daughter's face, through the striking resemblance of his eldest grandson. If the campesinos above El Limón had been made small by history, by massacres, by decrees, if they had been reduced by the extent of their own poverty, they were never diminished, the evidence suggests, in the eyes of Don Alberto. With his own sentence commuted, he was free to commute the sentences of others— to redefine the terms of their servitude, to liberalize their relations to the land.

About Lenora and her lover, Juan; about the singer María López and her rabble-rousing man, Santana; about Nicha, the maid, and her comically disgruntled husband, Tomas, Bill says, whenever I ask him, "They were like Tiburcio, Beth. They came with the land. Or at least their families did."

"So they were *bought,* then." I press.

"No. They were there when he bought the land. There is a difference."

"So they *became* his." I want to be very clear.

"It's just the way it was. They were living there, and he bought the land. They became part of what was his, of what he loved." Don Alberto maintained their houses—fortified the bricks, bought new tin for the roofs, supplied wood for the shrines and for the rafters and for the doors. He paid for their labor: terracing, planting, pruning, weeding, picking, year-round vigilance. He built a well in the courtyard beneath that big *papaturro* tree, wedged a figure of St. Anthony into an opening in the stone, and told them to come anytime with their empty jugs: *Save yourself the trip to the river; this water is clean and it is blessed.* During picking season, he turned the last room in his small brick house into a shop of sorts—stocked it with sausage and salted meats, corn and beans, candy, and sold it all at cost to the campesinos, who were constantly at risk for blowing a whole week's salary on a Saturday night of cheap *guaro.* At risk for forsaking dinner, shoes, their babies' medicines. At risk for an argument decided by machetes. Don Alberto sold the city stock to those whom he had paid with proper national currency while Tere, his wife, made change in a wooden box that now sits here, empty, next to me. Over time some fourteen families took their places at St. Anthony's Farm—cousins and distant aunts, godparents, brothers, sisters—some squeezing into the shacks already built, some constructing their own tight shelters and planting their own corn, hatching their own chickens, maybe even fattening their own pigs to hang from roof ledges in times of mourning.

"It sounds like one big, happy family," I say to Bill.

"No. Not always happy. Some drank like fools. They fought their fights. Lots of really bad stuff happened. But they were one family anyway, all of them somehow related."

In and of itself, such community making on a coffee hill was unremarkable, a by-product of discriminating laws and a burgeoning population. For the very late nineteenth-century land reform laws that had ushered in the coffee era had also displaced what remained of native towns and native centers, discarded a four-century tradition, however embattled, of agrarian communal lands. The laws stripped the Indians of the fields they'd worked together, left them vulnerable and landless, created a class of shell-shocked vagrants. With much of the land now held by just a handful of men, coffee farms would evolve into the country's new breed of rural village, where year-round workers housed their families on borrowed spits of earth and surrendered their labor for the privilege.

On many farms, across many hillsides, these squatters and tenants were seen as capital resources, to be deployed, as one deployed machines, for profit and social standing. But in Don Alberto's case, these people, at least the way I sift the evidence, became his friends. They taught him what they knew about the land. They made him their tortillas. They sliced bananas for his grandchildren and brought him fruit from his own trees. And when they grew sick with cholera, he brought them medicine. When they were orphaned, he bought them mattressed beds. When a tree branch snapped and split their skulls, he conveyed them to the city doctors, paid the bills. When they were old and their bodies no longer served their needs, he made sure they had their food, medicine, blankets, stood beside them at the end of day and remarked on the sun going down.

"You want a story I haven't told you about Lenora," Bill says, acknowledging the questions I've been asking on a Sunday afternoon. He averts his eyes, drops his bucket into memory's well. He has been battling a dull fever, and the house is sickly quiet. We have spoken of Lenora many times, but now I am asking him for more, asking for memories he hasn't thought to share, or hasn't wanted to. "Lenora, I suppose, was always there," he says, after time passes. "When we were kids, she was already really, really old, practically ancient. To tell the truth, we didn't like her much, and she definitely had no use for us. She was bitter, and we annoyed her like hell."

"You didn't like her?" I am startled. This is not the story I expected, not the sentiment for a slow, sickness-trampled day. "But she was blind, Bill." I use this well-known fact in her defense, remind my husband of what he's often said to me about this woman who predated Don Alberto at St. Anthony's, and who kept living in the house he built her long after he was gone. Her house is the one that faced his house across the court-yard. Each house built of brick, each roofed with Spanish tiles. She made tortillas; that was her specialty. She had a lover, Juan, whom she never married, but with whom she lived for maybe sixty years, or maybe even seventy.

"She might have been blind, but she was nasty," Bill asserts. "Or maybe she wasn't nasty. Maybe she just didn't like kids." I shake my head, still disbelieving. I have studied Bill's photographs of this Lenora, the white wisps of hair that escape her long, thick braid. Her neck is thin and withered. Her nose is broad and sound. The only lines on her face are the two deep, mouthlike grooves that form each edge of her firm cheeks. In whatever portrait I stare into, her eyes are gray, frozen, sightless, overbig. She seems vulnerable. She seems prone to mourning, silence. She seems to trust the young man with the camera, the man who is now my husband, who sits here with a fever in Pennsylvania and disturbs his wife with unexpected adjectives.

"What did she do that was so nasty?"

"She told on us."

"For what?"

"For everything. Like when we jumped on her roof, she told my grandfather."

"Well, geez, Bill, what were you doing on her roof?" I demand, suddenly imagining myself in the old blind woman's stead, her darkness in the high heat of day, the pummeling, inconsiderate attack of boys' feet overhead.

"It was a game," Bill says. "Just a game." And then he explains about the water tank Don Alberto had built to catch the rain, to keep fresh water running in the dry season. The tank was built several yards back from Lenora's house, Bill says, and a thin metal pipe ran through the canopy of trees, across Lenora's tile roof, and down to the courtyard her three-room house shared with Don Alberto's three-room house, the big starship tree blooming between. Bill and his brothers and his friends: they hung from the metal pipes like monkeys. Began at the water tank and inched their way down, hand over hand, until they could swing themselves up onto Lenora's roof. The Spanish tiles would sometimes crackle underfoot, snap loudly, and something would go skidding, and they'd hear blind Lenora roar for Don Alberto, and then his voice, telling them to get down.

"She was no fun," Bill says, after he furrows his brow at me as if he's shocked to find me sitting here, across a table from him, as if he's surprised to find himself plunked down in the drone of present time.

"Yeah. Well," I say. "No wonder. You were jumping on her roof."

"Then again, she was blind," Bill says, considering the obvious, rolling it back over in his mind. "And Juan was deaf. It could have been that she was nice before she had all those reasons to get bitter."

But then again, Bill says, the blindness was her own fault. Because Don Alberto had tried to save her. He had tried to tell her that there was a word for what was changing the way light entered through her eyes and that city doctors could remove the deteriorated lenses and stop the dizzying blur. She might have been sixty-five—about this Bill isn't precisely sure—when the cataracts began to haunt her vision. Sixty-five when the sun began to alarm her and Juan's face began to look back at her as if reflected from a river. Bill was just a baby then. He remembers the stories more than the event.

Those were the years, he says, when the third room of Lenora and Juan's three-room house was open to the courtyard, leaving it exposed to wind, dust, the curiosity of onlookers, putting everything she did and the mood she did it in out there, on display. The kitchen's three walls were a dirty brick brown. There was a tiny window, the size of a missing brick, up high, on the farthest wall.

Lenora's oven, a flat iron skillet over an open flame, lay along the right wall, and across from it stood a worn-down table and two chairs, their caning rubbing thin. On the far wall, where the brick-sized window was, were stashed, hung, and piled Lenora's most holy things: cooking tools and aprons and yellow brooms, tin plates and jelly jars, water gourds, *cantaros*, the *metate,* the *comal*, the skewers, a row of five misshapen spoons hung on the rusted heads of nails banged into the wall. From the dark, smoked ceiling fell hooked sausage links and salted meats, and from the floor rose up baskets of sweet corn, a pile of worn grinding stones, buckets of raw, chestnut-brown beans. These were the things Lenora best understood. These were the comforts of her life.

On any given day she could be seen, so the stories go, bent over her one table, her slender hands in a limey pail of tortilla paste. She could be seen heaving the paste out of the pail onto the table, taking a breath, exhaling, and then beginning the slamming, the slapping, the folding and readying of the dough. Air would expand and then escape the white-yellow stuff. When the dough was right, she'd gather a palm's worth into one fist, and then she'd start shaping—patting and smoothing and pounding it down into its thick, unpocked circle. Onto the grill it went when it was good and ready, and then her hands made another, and sometimes her hair streamed down her back: loose and long toward her bare and narrow feet. One tortilla after another, thrown into the smoke of the grill.

She cooked tortillas in her kitchen. She cooked *pupusas* and squirrel, young chicken livers, fried plantains. She'd slipped the skins off bananas and mangoes to please her lover. She'd listen to the music the hard red beans made as they shifted in the burlap bags that clotted up her floor, and then she'd melt the beans together, spice them hot with garlic and onion, cook them with fat slabs of lard until they were gritty. She worked in smoke. She smelled of smoke. Her hair was smokey colored. When the cataracts wouldn't stop weaving their webs across her eyes, she agreed to go with Don Alberto in his jeep to the city, to city doctors who, he told her, knew the cure. *You are not to cook until your eyes are healed,* Don Alberto told Lenora, after the doctors were done and he'd brought her home and walked her to her door. *Promise me that you'll keep your face out of that smoke.* But Lenora was a woman of the kitchen. Her hands knew little save tortillas. She made the fire, the kitchen smoked, her raw eyes grew rawer still, instead of better. Frightened of the ghosts that soon crept back up into her eyes, she went to what she knew this time and found the local *curandero.*

I imagine her going down the hill to her magic man on the last day she'd ever see: the trees, the birds, the ground, the sky; the next day they would be gone. He would be old, as *curanderos* typically are, and he would have earned his reputation for scaring spirits and relieving the Siguanaba fever, for fixing the inexplicable miseries of muscles and of blood. His medicine shop would be like something flipped upside down and backwards, with a grove of herbs and dried grasses and garlic sprouting wildly from the ceiling—*hoja del golpe* to lessen bruise pain, *alhucema* to pacify babies, *mata niguas* for chigger flea sores—and incense and candles and glass jars of yellow goop lighting the floor like so many lanterns. The yellow goop contained the secrets of a charlatan. The promise of unghosted sight.

Lenora would have been shown the cot.

Lenora would have laid herself down.

She would have sipped the coffee the *curandero* offered, certain that it was the beginning of the cure. She would have accepted whatever thin tunes he had hummed, whatever chants steamed from his lips, however many times he circled in his dancing way the room's one dingy cot. And if he had placed two cloves of garlic on her eyes, she would have blessed the offering, and when he told her that the time had come, she would have brushed the cloves away, rolled back her eyelids, and trusted. She would have looked into the medicine man's black and deviant eyes, snapped that picture in her mind, inhaled her final, blurry vision. She would have said to herself: *Tomorrow: No more ghosts.* She would have submitted to the cure.

No one ever found out what the *curandero* poured into the vial that he emptied into old Lenora's eyes. No one, not even Don Alberto, when he went in rage to the mutilator and demanded a confession. But how could Lenora not have screamed when its fire singed her eye flesh? How could she not have panicked with the pain? How could she not have fractured deep inside when she realized—Was it sudden? Was it slow?— what had been taken from her life? Weeks later, Don Alberto's doctor took a pencil and tapped it, hard, against both Lenora's eyes, confirming what they all already knew. Lenora was blind. Her eyes were hard as marbles. Her hands alone would do the cooking now, forced to remember all that the eyes had taught them across so many tortilla years.

Unable to see, Lenora knew one taste best, and that was bitter. Unable to see, she now tossed her buckets of kitchen slop to the courtyard—fierce, wild arcs of filth—and did not care who might have met up with the waste. Unable to see, she found the sound of birds and wind, the sound of the oxcart, the sounds of a boy's shoes overhead unbearably close. She would at times neglect her braid and let her hair fall in its white streams down her back. She would hover near the smell of smoke. She would grow afraid to leave the kitchen. And when a shade tree fell the wrong way during pruning season and its heaviest limb found Juan smack in its path, she would be lucky not to see how her lover's skull had been banged apart, how it had split in two like ripened fruit.

Her eyeballs glassy to the touch, Lenora would soon know only that Juan had gone deaf because she had gone blind, that they would live out their lives now with two lost senses. And when Juan was at last gone, the people of St. Anthony's got him a box and laid him in it and came to lead his widow barefoot, to her lover's final moments in the sun—through the smoke of her kitchen and across to the courtyard gate, then up the road and to the path that ascends and empties into that sea of aqua crosses. She would climb her way up, climb up blindly behind the box, and she would stand among the turkeys, the crepe paper, the plastic leis, the songs, the families who lived and died together on that farm. They would sink Juan into the soil. They'd plant a cross up by his head. And when the sun had set, they would take Lenora by the hand and lead her back to the three-walled kitchen and the smoke of her tortillas.

Lenora, as photographed by Bill

CERTAINTY

⸺⧉⸺

*T*he odd thing is that I am certain I met Lenora. Odder still, Bill is certain that I did not. "That first trip to the farm," I say, I insist, "I saw her sitting there. In one of those broken chairs. Outside that kitchen. There was a mutt sniffing for scraps between her feet." I rally with more images. More particulars. More witnessing. "Her hair was loose," I say to Bill, "and she was wearing pink, and I am sure, I'm really sure, that when you took me inside to see the old tortilla grill, you said, 'These *are* Lenora's spoons. This *is* her bucket.' Present tense."

"But didn't she die the year we got there? Right before we arrived? In March, maybe, or April?" Bill doesn't accuse and he doesn't exhort. He merely tries to isolate the truth.

"She died afterwards," I say, certain about this too, the knowledge seeded in a separate memory. "Nora called in the fall, don't you remember? Nora called to tell you that she was gone."

"I remember Nora calling," Bill says softly. "But I can't remember when."

"Well, I saw Lenora, Bill," I say. "I have this picture in my mind. This perfect picture. Her white hair. Her faded dress. Her back so straight on that broken wooden chair."

"But do you have a *photograph*?" Bill says. "You'd have taken a photograph if you'd met her. You would have, wouldn't you?"

"Well maybe. I don't know. But I know I saw her. That's what matters."

Still, just to be safe, I tramp up to the attic, fling wide the dusty door, and haul my photo boxes to the light. On the floor in my son's room, I sit poring through negatives and albums and hundreds of loose prints, eager for my evidence, my *see here*, the can't-be-refuted. The search yields nothing save some overexposed shots of an empty chair, a scruffy dog, five spoons hanging like sentries from their nails. I search again. Bill strokes my hair. I wonder what he thinks of me, this wife seeking authority over the life her husband's lived.

"This doesn't prove anything," I say to Bill, after I've searched through the confounding piles a third time, shoved them aside. "Just because she isn't here doesn't mean I didn't meet her. Right?" But the truth is, I am worried. I am disgusted with my mind. It occurs to me that in my quest to know my husband, to transport myself into his history and see, I have lost some barrier reef in me, dispensed with the sane, essential filter between what I've been told and what I've witnessed.

Were memory an organ, I would curse it, but it is not; memory is a marvel of extroverted dendrites and clever networks, of triggers and choreography. Experience is sight, sound, smell, taste, the burn of muscles, the precipitance of words, the rise of passion, the chill of regret. Experience involves the whole brain, excites neurons across the cerebrum, is stored not in a single place but in dissociated fragments. What gets remembered over time gets remembered because of the connections forged between scattered encoded neurons. Remembering is about reassembling those connections, and about forgetting, *strategically* forgetting so much that lies between, and the more we reassemble our memories—the more we shape them or confide them or defend them or make them our art—the truer they seem to us, the more certain and more bedrock. Our memories tell us who we have been and therefore who we are. They are the stories we whisper to ourselves. They are the irreplaceable, irreducible, irrepressible impositions of order over the chaos of our lives.

And yet: The neural mechanisms that give us memory are similar—mischievously, wickedly, frustratingly similar—to those that stoke the fires of imagination. No memory is absolute or foolproof or complete. What we retrieve is not always fact. What we forget is part of our fiction.

The first conversation I ever had with my husband was about El Salvador, about his past. His stories have become the habit with us—his childhood photos the ones I study, his memories the ones I tap. He asks me little about where I come from, asks to see no photographs, does not take his son to his side and say, confidingly, *Now here's a story about your mom.* Years ago, Bill concluded that the suburbia of my youth was as benign as the suburbia we now live in, and I have conceded this when he has said as much, admitted that I never chased a cat-sized butterfly, never watched a war play out down the street, never danced over the head of a woman who'd gone blind, never presumed to make a scorpion a pet. Still, I say, it was my childhood, it was where I came from, my own adventure, however quiet. Guilty, I say this, hoping for a question, hoping to be wondered about. But Bill looks back and sees the tangled trees of a coffee farm, the shadow of Siguanaba, the sudden violent hues of birds, the praying mantis alert on the head of Don Alberto, and then looks at me and sees suburban streets, suburban friendships, suburban skies, a mulched, well-mannered garden. It was an accident, Bill's falling in love with me. It was a risk, binding himself up in marriage to an American girl, a suburban girl so entirely naïve that she thought she'd be somehow big enough to hold him.

And he has been faithful, and he has been gentle, and he has been generous and dear, but still: the adventures of his country go on without him. The adventures are what I cannot give him, what I nevertheless still try to give him—with photographs, with stories, with the stones I meticulously find, then polish so as to give them to our son.

Bill is today the only man I would ever wish to marry. He is calm and intelligent and immaculately honest. He remembers the roses I love and brings home forty for a birthday. He saves everything he's earned and slips a diamond on my finger. He makes his art and lets it be; he combs his hand through my dark hair; he sits with me when I feel too all alone until the loneliness is liberated, then forgotten. He says, *I love you*, and something shattered heals, something missing is restored, something necessary is salvaged. He is a father like no other, as proud as I am of our son, and this small house aches when he is gone; the mood is less resilient and more hollow. And yet, Bill is never really all the way home, here in America. He is never completely settled on this temperate suburban ground.

Over and again I have been sitting here or lying near when a sound has sent him back—a sound, or the intensity of the color blue, or a mango bleeding its mottled juice onto a porcelain plate. Bill peels an orange and he remembers Juan scrambling up a tree, plucking a fat one, knifing off its rind with a filthy blade, offering the blackened orange up. *I ate it, because what could I do? This was his gift. By then he was deaf as a stone.* He takes our son out jeeping on pocked dirt roads because this was how he did it as a kid. He perceives that the rain has kicked itself into a storm and steeps his mind with its stored images of road-swallowing monsoons. Bill is here in America, and so he keeps his foreign history close, while I, living near the places I have always lived, grow dull to the distinctions of my past, am not asked to tell a story.

And now: I want Bill and his brothers and Nora and Adela to know more about their histories than they do. And now: I persist. I ask. I supplement. It is me phoning the antique book stores and begging for their stock of Salvador texts, their flirty coffee pamphlets. It is me consulting the resurrected maps, reconciling the contradictions in the books, knitting the family history into the country's broader tempest, and chasing the chimera of the unbroken narrative. It is me calling my husband in the middle of the day to protest the *matanza*, to deliver the news of plate tectonics, to rail against the indigo, to mourn lost cocoa trees. My facts do not disturb him, do not modulate his memory. He knows what he knows, what he has willed himself to know. He is there, inside the land he left, and I am not there, *I am nowhere* in his incubated memory, even when the facts should place me there, even when I am polishing these stones.

I want to tell a single story. I want my husband to look back and keep looking until he finds me inside the things he loves, the country that shaped him, the memories that keep him whole. I put myself there—imagining while he remembers— and suddenly I don't know the facts, I don't know if I met Lenora once upon that hill, or if I simply, truly, loved her, *learned* to love her, because of my husband's tales. For an instant I am certain that I know nothing, that it is hopeless, and then, the next instant, I am spared by the most obvious of reprieves: Bill calls his mother. Calls and asks the simple question. *Lenora?* Nora says. *Well.* And now the phone goes silent as Nora counts backwards, reassembles all those memories of her own. I wait. Bill waits. Nora remembers. *Lenora's been gone eleven years,* she finally calculates. Eleven. Which means that I didn't meet her once but twice, on a second trip, as well. That what is missing among my photographs *is* the evidence, after all. *Because that was the year,* Nora goes on, the dendrites crackling now, the thin connections growing a little less thin and less transparent, Bill translating, *when that bee stung my horse and he went crazy on the hills. Remember? When he went flying down the road that drops so quickly on the farm and there was nothing to do but to throw myself off the saddle. That was the year, yes, that was the month when Lenora died, because my leg had been shattered and I couldn't make it to the funeral, and when I finally got back to the farm, she was gone. Eleven years. I'm certain.*

If I cannot place my faith in the images I do not have, I can still—can I not?—trust the photographs that slouch in my over-taxed boxes, in my albums, that come in as unwieldy attach-ments over email. The photos that I have taken. The ones that I have borrowed. The ones that I have begged for. Bill's stash. The images that testify to what's been lost, and who.

There is in my collection a photograph of Don Alberto's Santa Tecla house, just one, which Adela's son Richard sent to me. It is a beautiful house, so American southern plantation in its style that I am always newly taken aback until I remember that it had been sent to El Salvador in pieces from the States. In the photograph, the house is encircled by an iron fence but not obliterated by it. Its windows are caught in eyebrow-shaped insets, or set off running, ladder like, up the expanses of the stucco; its roofs are peaked and prominent but lack pretension. The photo is not, strictly speaking, black-and-white, it's more sepia hued, and the house catches an aggressive sun without get-ting scorched by it, or faded. One sleeping porch is revealed up high, and there's a gracious, airy porch below, and there are so many leaves and flowers entwined about the fence's iron spikes that it is impossible to guess the species or the season of the year.

This is the house where Tiburcio built his most famous garden, where that oddball nut tree grew, and where Bill lived, as he says, among the leaves of a fecund tangerine tree. This is where Tere's roses were and her jasmine, the sporadica of exotic orchids, the pheasants on the side yard and the parakeets in their cages in the back. There was a pool of water in which red-bellied minnows swam, and Bill remembers watching Don Alberto go out among his wild menagerie. *He'd take old bread and mix it with milk, he'd mash tortillas, he'd go into the garden. Most of that stuff he fed the birds. The leftovers were tossed to the minnows.*

The photo leaves me knocking on its door. I can't go inside until Bill escorts me. "Now, that was a house," Bill says. "That was such a great house," and, eager to amble, he walks me through it, room by room, suggests how long and wide and high the rooms were, and how many rooms in all: two living rooms, two kitchens, one restaurant-sized dining room, the maids' suite, the master bedroom, the other bedrooms, one after the other. "He liked to pace," Bill says, referring, of course, to his grandfather, "and the house let him go on and on in a straight line and back." Doors would be opened and shut, and Don Alberto would walk miles in his house.

Imported and erected under the supervision of Santa Tecla's richest family, the house had had two lives before Don Alberto bought it. First it had served as the home of one of the infamous Guirolas, the brothers who, along with a few other wealthy entrepreneurs, were chiefly responsible for converting Santa Tecla into an expanse of coffee trees. The municipality, largely a natural forest in the mid-nineteenth century, had some two million coffee trees in production by 1882 as part of the Guirola legacy; the family's large and efficient processing plant was overseen by Angel Guirola's own two daughters. The Guirolas owned cattle haciendas and invested in the railway and participated in the machinations of the banks, and in the middle of the town, facing Santa Tecla's prettiest park, they put their money on display in the form of three imposing houses—importing neoclassical arches, columns, cornices, balustrades, and, in the case of that one singular house my husband loved, the éclat of the American South.

When the Guirolas tired of the plantation-style house, they made it over into a gentleman's club, erecting tennis courts where Tiburcio's garden would someday be and serving lavish meals within. Its wood floors and high, tin ceilings, its peaked roofs and genteel porches were a Salvadoran anomaly, an elitist's calling card, but by the 1950s there were other clubs and other hot spots, other watering holes for wealth. The club went on the market, and, with almost twenty years of coffee profits, Don Alberto bought it for himself. Bought it from the family that had once paid him to administer one of their cattle haciendas, from the family whose bank had given him the loan with which he acquired the beginnings of St. Anthony's Farm. It was, without question, still an entirely one-of-a-kind house, and Don Alberto and Tere and their family and their maids only ever lived in its bottom half, Don Alberto taking his daily constitutional through the concatenation of downstairs rooms while his grandchildren explored the five fabulous rejected rooms above.

"Christ," Bill says, thinking back. "It was great up there. It was our playground. Full of nostalgia, full of his things, stuff from the thirties, all these miniature photographs." It was just trunks of stuff put down without any thought given to decor or order, as if the huge, elegant suite of rooms was merely attic space, leftover. Bill and his brothers—they went through everything, Bill says: the old coins, the old medicines, the old bottles, all the boxes. "We'd pretend we were scientists and mix the gunk inside the bottles. Once, I remember, I invented ink. I put it into all my pens. God knows what it was. Probably toxic." And once, Bill says, he found a pair of cockfighting knives, little threatening arcs of steel that had been tied to doomed birds' legs.

"Your grandfather did *cockfighting*?" I ask Bill, conveying my disgust with this new and wholly unwelcome bit of biography.

"I don't know if he fought his own birds," Bill says, never a sentimentalist, and not one to soften a picture. "But the cockfighting arena was just down the street, right on the corner. I'm sure he went."

But Bill's favorite room in the house, he says, was—hands down—the attic, which could be reached only by climbing a tall, skinny ladder and flipping the trapdoor open overhead. "Hot as hell in there," Bill says. "God, it was hot. But there was this one window at the other end of it that was used to vent the house. It was like this big achievement, fighting all that heat and not being able to breathe, and finally getting to the window and catching whatever breeze." Like breaking the surface of water after a long submergence in the sea. And in the attic there were all these pigeons that had flown in, and once, among the pigeons, Bill discovered the skeleton of a bat. And, as if the attic and the tangerine tree and the trunks were not enough, there was another favorite place, Bill says: the sleeping porch; it was frivolous, an add-on. It's where Bill and his brothers and his friends would go to watch the car races and the go-cart competitions that encircled his grandfather's block.

The house faced the prettiest park, Bill always says this. And one brother lived down the street in one direction, and two more of Don Alberto's six siblings lived another two blocks in another direction, in the house their parents had left them in; they had no choice. Francisco and María. Together and unhappy. Living in a home I've always thought of as the House of the Walking Dead. Traditional Spanish colonial. Harsh wall to the outside. Bars over the windows. A courtyard so overgrown, so weedy, that the interior got no light.

Bill tells me the end of the siblings' story. I secretly imagine the start, taking María first, because it is easier to empathize, easier to picture the bride-to-be getting ready for the wedding. She must have been pretty; all the Bondanzas are. She must have been deeply in love with the man who had asked her to be his wife.

"How did he die again?"

"A car accident. I think it was a car accident."

"How old was she then?"

"No more than twenty."

"But she stayed in love."

"She never put away her wedding dress. She never married. Ana Ruth was still driving her to the fiancé's grave when I was in college and she was eighty."

Two lives lost, I always think. The groom and the bride who wouldn't forsake him. Don Alberto's oldest sibling condemned to more than sixty years of mourning, condemned to live longer than Bill's grandfather, even, in that house that got no light because the courtyard had no gardener. And when it came her turn to pass on, she wouldn't go easily; she lay delirious in her bed for weeks, lay there entertaining visions while her maid sat bedside in an uncomfortable chair. Murmuring and tossing, sweating and chilling, opening her eyes and gesturing wildly, then closing her eyes, catching a stanza of sleep, only to, abruptly, roll her eyelids back again and emphatically reach toward the great middle distance. After so many weeks of sitting there, wondering what it was that her mistress saw, the maid finally turned around to see. It was a man in a white uniform, military dress, a gentle face. Standing there, clear as day in the dark to the maid, who muffled her scream when she saw it.

"So the groom came at last?"

"No. Not the groom. It was my grandfather. He'd passed away a few years before. He'd come, they say, to take his shattered sister home."

"What happened?"

"The maid wouldn't sit there anymore at night. They got a nurse, and my great aunt died shortly after."

As for Francisco? He had died a few years earlier, his death discovered by the maid's son, Rubén, who was just a little kid, Bill says, when he opened Francisco's bedroom door and stumbled onto the suicide. "What I remember about Francisco is that he dressed with tremendous formality—little hats and oversized suits, looking like a throwback to the forties," Bill says. "But he was so small, and he was terribly introverted, which everyone always blamed on how he'd been born three months too early."

Francisco was the youngest of the seven, and when he came too soon, they built him a wooden box and fitted it out with a light bulb, and hoped the light would keep him warm until he was big enough for the world. Like his oldest sister, he never married. Like her, he never left his parents' house, living in one wing off the unkempt courtyard while María nursed her wedding reveries across the way. How often the two crossed paths, nobody is certain. Whether they sat together at meals or ate separately in their bedrooms is still a matter of debate among those who should have known. What Francisco did for a living is contested, too. In my mind, I have made him haunted by the *matanza*, which would have struck when he was in his early twenties, which might have chased him even more completely into his head and made him powerless, made him *feel* powerless. But that's conjecture. All that is known is that Francisco was a lonely man, a man in perfect suits and perfect hats, a man his brothers protected and supported over a lifetime. All that is known is that one day little Rubén, the maid's lonely only son, went off looking for Francisco and found the mess of him in his bedroom. Rat poison, Bill says. Imagine what it does to you, he says. Imagine what it was like for Rubén to find the man of that house that way.

There are no photographs in my possession of María and Francisco. There is no proof that I met Lenora on the farm. There are those we've never known but think we do, and those we might have met, but can't recall, and houses we can't enter but have walked through. Imagination is like memory, and memory is not the truth, and there are ghosts in this story that I tell; there are guardian angels; there is the roaring sadness of broken and vanished things. I do my best with what I persuade myself I know. I try to find what my husband's lost, and give it back to him.

Greetings on the road to coffee

BLOOD LINES

⸺◦◦◦⸺

*T*he summer Jeremy was born, Nora came to our house and stayed for a time while I failed—miserably—at being who she'd hoped I'd be. I failed, first of all, because Nora had wanted a granddaughter, not a grandson, and I failed, second of all, because I hoarded this boy who had been born to me—hoarded the smell and feel and weight of him, planted him in his own crib at night and sang him to sleep with my songs. American songs with American words. My mother's passed-on lullabies wafting through his channeled ear. It was so horribly hot that summer, so horribly unrelieved, and every day my husband went to work and every day I disappointed my mother-in-law in ways that cannot be emended. I loved my Jeremy. I held him, steadfastly, in my arms. I was home, in my country, on my soil, with my son. I sang him my American songs.

But no matter how suburban and protected my baby was, no matter how Ivy League and graceful his father, no matter how influential and loving my own all-American parents, there was no denying the exotic look Jeremy had about his eyes, or the slight hint of darkness in his skin, or the blackness of his hair that wallowed, from the beginning, past his ears. There was something foreign about Jeremy from the start. There was his father's blood that would not be negated, and the Salvadoran bibs that had arrived in plastic sleeves, and the Salvadoran linens, embroidered collars. There were the Salvadoran songs that somehow did get sung, and the endearments: *bonito niño, buen niño, mucho gusto bonito niño.* The slip of Spanish into a child's ear. The electrochemical sparks of another language.

*T*he first time we took Jeremy to El Salvador, he was four. It was February 1993, just one year into the cease-fire that had been cobbled together by an exhausted government and a depleted gang of rebels. I didn't like the idea of going to a place still percolating with the memory of an eleven-year civil war, and fought it. Aimless death squads, I cautioned. Choleric guerrillas. One percent of the population sacrificed to the fighting, their tangled, splintered, naked bones still barely hidden underground, or not hidden at all, but dumped inside mass graves. I argued that it was indecent, irresponsible to take a child to that place, that cease-fires had been marched out before in El Salvador but discontent had a mind of its own. *Safety is here. The familiar is here. The things he's grown accustomed to. All here.* I argued, and of course I lost. A son should know where his father comes from. What he means when he says, Once upon a time I was a boy.

Jeremy was four. He liked cars, and he liked planes. I equipped him with a bag full of his favorite miniatures and did not let him out of sight for five protracted days. In the photographs of that trip that year, Jeremy rides the proud shoulders of his father and, sometimes, the shoulders of Rodi and Mario, Bill's brothers. On occasion he wears the thin plastic helmet that he favored at the time, its imagined protection jammed down over his ears, its green plastic visor snapped forward over his eyes. He wears the shirts and overalls I loved dressing him in, comports himself in the chubby feathery cheeks that I'm addicted, still, to touching. I am not in any of the photographs, but Jeremy is there and, again, he is there: in the arms of his father and his father's country.

Every marriage, my friend Sandy says, is a multicultural marriage. I think that's true and right. My mother's mother was Irish and her father was Italian; they learned, over a lifetime, to mix the spices. Bill's parents were from separate places—the United States, El Salvador; they remained in separate places all their lives. Couples I know grew up one rural and the other urban, one Orthodox Jew and the other lapsed Catholic, one Canadian and the other a pure shot of Manhattan, one bothered and the other meditatively calm. There are no perfect photographs, there are only photographs, only evidence of the ways we dance, in and out, in and out, of one another. It is in the ways we love our children that they learn just how to love, and whom to love, and what family history is.

In 1993, in the wake of a depleted civil war, Jeremy saw his father's country for the first, astonishing time. He saw the marketplace crammed with the fruits he couldn't name and the radishes arranged like Christmas wreaths and the bulbs of scallions, fat as fists. He saw the babies on the streets in their cardboard boxes, the weathered ladies behind their mounds of dried bouquets, the men who would pose for my camera, and the woman who would not, though I snapped her picture anyway, a portrait of disdain. Jeremy rode on the shoulders of the men of Santa Tecla, and saw the place, which had become a mall, where Don Alberto's plantation-style house had stood, saw the park, now so run down, where colones had been tossed out to the wind, saw what his father taught him to see: *See the feathers of this bird? They have a story. See the pig on the street? It's someone's dinner. See these orange fruits? When I was a kid, when I was a boy, I'd climb the trees and eat them.* Jeremy was shouldered all over

Santa Tecla, and the next day he was shouldered through the port town of La Libertad, rode high among salted fish and pinkened two-day-old snapper, among buckets of octopus and platters of shark, among the merchants and their children and the vagrants on the pier that stretches out into the restless Pacific that almost swallowed Don Alberto whole.

The third day we drove to Panchimalco and found a girl hidden coyly in the trees. She wore a clean white dress and dirty feet, and she was singing to herself while she pumped into the air on a makeshift ropy swing, and then all of the sudden she was singing to her brother, who had materialized, as if out of nowhere, from behind the trees. In Panchimalco there was a boy who gave his sister a bath while her underpants bleached whiter on a line above their heads, and there was another boy, dressed in a school uniform, sitting priestly and contemplative by the cathedral's locked-shut door. Jeremy rode high on his father's shoulders in Panchimalco and on his uncle's shoulders, too, as Bill and Rodi walked side by side and I walked in their shadows. I reached up. I held my child's hand. I listened to the Spanish that was kinship between brothers.

What are you talking about?

I'll tell you later.

What are you thinking?

How pretty it is here.

On the fourth day we went to the farm. Went up there to have a party, and everybody came. Bill's brothers and childhood friends, their mothers, his aunts, Nicha and Selena, the entire cast of Tupperware. Salvadoran weather is calming in February. The coffee cherries are gone; there is something of a breeze. We ate lunch on the porch of Don Alberto's brick house, looked out on the house where Lenora had once cooked tortillas blind. Nicha's daughter was the cook this time. Nicha's grandson delivered the meal on clean white porcelain. Everybody ate and I took pictures, never letting my son out of my sight.

Afterwards the women formed a circle and they talked, trading recent cease-fire horrors for entertainment, hitting their thighs with their manicured hands as they exclaimed and sighed and goaded one another on. Adela, sitting beside me, directed the traffic of their talk, putting her hand up frequently to stop the noisy flow so that she could turn and make it English, make it make sense for me.

"They stopped me at the stop sign and then they jumped into my car," one said.

"They put a gun up to my face and tore the gold cross from my neck," said another.

"I was going to a party, see? They stole everything, including—hands up—the rings right off my fingers."

"No."

"I was afraid to leave the house."

"It was so frightening."

"I was afraid to drive my car."

"As was I; I hardly drove."

"I didn't have a choice. I went to the bank. I got the money for my workers. But they waited until my purse was full, and they got me from behind, and then they banged me on the head. Ay, my head. Ay. Ay. My head."

"Do you like my little country?" Adela turned at last and said. I shook my head one way and then the other. Adela laughed. The others laughed, too. Someone went to get more rum. Nora opined that it was time for a siesta.

The next day was the final day, and there was another party planned. This one would take place at Nora's city house, and everyone had dressed the part. Rafael's children and Chepe's children and Jamie's children, and the mothers and the aunts and the grandmothers: they wore their tailored clothes, their maid-pressed linens, the hair that had been coifed for the purpose of the party earlier on. They wore their best clothes, and they smashed a stick against a swinging, bruised piñata, and they divided into even teams to play a drawbridge game. The oldest of them all was Don Alberto's widow, Tere. Still thin and still quite elegant, her white hair tending, in a certain light, toward quiet hints of blue. She wore a pearl-colored blouse with gold stitching at its collar, and it seemed to me, as I studied her, that she wore a fallen crown. *Once,* Bill told me. *Once. They found a trunk full of letters Don Alberto wrote her. Love letters. Very romantic. Once,* Bill told me. *Once. My grandfather and my grandmother were very much in love. Can you tell, looking at her now, how beautiful she was?*

"What do you think of my little country?" Adela came to where I was sitting and asked, her cigarette cocked away from her smile. "What do you think of our parties?"

"Bueno."

"Sí. Ay, Beth. Listen to you."

"What?"

"Listen to you, speaking our Spanish."

The kids were singing a Spanished "London Bridge Is Falling Down." They were hammering the piñata, and offering Jeremy the stick. And then all of the sudden they were singing "Happy Birthday" to my son, who was still months away from being five. He looked at me. I looked, smiling, back. Adela, pretty as a movie star, exhaled a plume of smoke and sighed.

"What do you remember about that first trip to Dad's country?" I ask Jeremy now, when it's just the two of us, the two of us and all these pictures on the floor.

"I remember the party best," he says, after thinking for a while.

"Which one?"

"The party that they threw me."

"You mean the piñata party? At Nora's Santa Tecla house?"

"Yeah. That one. When it was me and all those second cousins and they sang me 'Happy Birthday.'"

"What do you remember best about it?"

"Nothing really. Nothing much."

"Then why do you think you remember it?"

"Because everyone had come."

Tiburcio

DEPARTURE

———∞∞∞———

*T*hey came for Don Alberto's dying, too—the entire town, Bill says, all the campesinos from the farm. This is the story that he doesn't like to tell. This is the end, and words can't change it. This is the sickness no one could ever cure.

"He was traveling in Europe," Bill will tell me when I ask, a quiet voice, all gravity. The eyes turned away, toward the past, the country that still lies between us.

"Alone?" I speak as softly as I can.

"With Nora and Rodi. With Adela's daughter, Beca."

"When?" A whisper in his ear. A kiss.

"August. 1976."

"What was the first sign?"

"He was tired."

"What were the other signs?"

"He'd grown much too thin too quickly."

"What did they do?"

"They flew him to Miami. For tests."

"Then?"

"They flew him to New Orleans. More tests."

"What happened afterwards?"

"They flew him to El Salvador."

"They knew he was dying?"

"Yes."

"It was stomach cancer?"

"Yes."

"What did you do?"

"I stayed home."

By which Bill means that he got on a plane and flew to the States, where he was scheduled to start his sophomore year. De-boarded, made his way to the university campus, withdrew from all his classes, left no indication, no explanation for his friends, just disappeared. Returned to the airport, took the next flight home, hardly left the side of the man he'd loved so fiercely his life long, loved as he loves his son today, with that much force and passion.

*T*hose who can visit come to visit. They stream their way to the great house in Santa Tecla that was once a private club and preposterously boasted of the American South. They stream their way there and wait in the exotic orchid garden or in the rooms with the ceilings that went way up high, and they wait their turn, like so many sinners bound for confession. They wait to speak to Don Alberto, to sit in chairs behind their steaming brews of black-sugar sweetened coffee while the great man sits with them, still capable of chairs, and then, later, not capable of chairs, he reclines against the sofa and, later, does not leave the bed. The campesinos and the city folk. The old men and the young ones. The former maids and their children and their children too, and the distant relatives, and the son he fathered, yes, there was a son he fathered before Nora and Ana Ruth and Martha and Adela and Beto, before he married Tere: that son comes too. They all come, and he receives them one by one, while Bill worries, and Mario and Rodi worry, and certainly the others worry, too, that he is ebbing too quickly, letting himself go less corporeal with each *hola,* each rubbing touch of the hand, each memory that he makes for them and leaves to them, in passing. Maybe already he wants to be way up in the hills. Maybe already he dreams of the parakeets that slice the sky or the crop he will not see complete itself with cherries.

I can take you up to St. Anthony's, Bill tells him. Or doesn't tell him. That part is not remembered. I can take you up to St. Anthony's, Bill wants to tell him. I can take you into your own silent place. Away from other people's memories, away from all those waiting, still, to say goodbye.

But Don Alberto is sicker now and the sickness smell steals through his skin, fumes from his lungs, is persistent; he is too weak to travel. The maids palm antiseptics into every surface, spray the house with the acrid stink of Lysol, walk as quietly as they can in their rubber shoes. The maids go in and out, and the children, the grandchildren go in, rarely come out, and then there is a new knock at the door. It is Hilario Peñate, an outlaw braving the consequences to see his former friend.

So you are going to go now, Hilario Peñate says, when he is standing bedside, a big man hovering over a much too small one. *I heard you were dying.*

Hilario Peñate, Bill's grandfather says, whispers maybe, extends a hand. *My God. Hilario Peñate.*

"Who?" I ask Bill now. "Who?"

"Wait," Bill says, and he finds the man's picture in the picture books—Hilario Peñate holding my husband high, July 20, 1958. In the photo, it is Bill's first birthday and his feet are nudged up against the big man's pistol-loaded holster, his little face, which looks like Jeremy's face, which also looks like his grandfather's face, just inches away from the outlaw's jowl. "Hilario Peñate. Remember? I told you. My grandfather's right-hand man for twenty years, maybe thirty. His administrator, in charge of all of the farms. The man he trusted with the growing and the picking, with the land he owned. He was the one."

"When you were growing up?"

"No. He was gone when I was growing up."

"Where did he go?"

"He disappeared."

"Why did he go?"

"Because he had a lot of enemies, and because one of his enemies tried to kill him. Somewhere up at the farm, I don't know where, and I was too young to remember now exactly when."

"Hilario Peñate," I turn his name over with my tongue. "Hilario Peñate."

"It's a funny story," Bill says. "A funny sad story. Because Peñate's assassin waited for Peñate behind a ledge of dirt. Somewhere near the side of some road he crouched and waited for Peñate to ride by."

"And then?"

"And then when Peñate finally came as the assassin knew he would, the guy stood up and shot at him, but the bullet ricocheted off of the dirt ledge. Peñate pretended to die, that was the thing. Fell down dramatically from his horse, and the guy who thought he'd shot him went to take a shit. He was busy with his business when Peñate, his horse now tied to a tree, his big feet quiet in the bushes, lifted the loaded pistol from his holster and shot the shitting assassin point-blank. The news made its way quickly to the national guard, and the guard started hunting for Peñate, and when my grandfather heard that there was a bounty on his friend's head, he went into the hills and he found him and he warned him: *You'll be caught. You have to leave. You have to leave right now.*"

"So your grandfather never heard from Peñate again?"

"No. Not until when he was dying."

"And you never saw Peñate again?"

"Not until he came that day. No. And never after that."

"What were you thinking, when you realized it was him?"

"I was thinking that he had the sweetest face, this really sweet and gentle face that didn't belong with the hands of a murderer."

So you're going to go now.

I heard you were dying, and I came.

And then they hugged one another, the administrator and his boss, and Peñate took a chair and started to speak of life in exile. Bill left them to themselves, Bill says. He left it in a private place, these two men's last goodbye.

*D*on Alberto died one month to the day that they'd discovered he was dying. He died anchored into the hands of those he loved and into the memories of others, died, but not before he'd made his peace, saying to Bill: *I have confidence in you. Take care of your brothers.* Don Alberto died and I imagine, because Bill imagines, that he died thinking of the farm, thinking that you could always trust the land, you could always depend on things to grow. Sit in the shade and watch blossoms give way to the green that will soon give way to cherries.

They honored him at St. Anthony's Church, where he hadn't gone in some thirty years. They said their prayers and lit their candles, and then drove his body north. It was a long black hearse. It was morning, early September. They were the only traffic, they were what moved through the streets as the crowds gathered around and pressed tremulously close. The people from the neighborhood who wore their Sunday suits. The people from the hills who had heard the news and started out at dawn to walk the miles, their shoes hung about their necks to save them for the procession. In the streets of Santa Tecla, they stood together, undivided, while the long black hearse pulled through, and above, beyond, in the towering distance, parakeets threw themselves against the sky and trees took their morning sips of sun. And then it was men, my husband among them, who conveyed Don Alberto's casket to its grave in the heart of the city. Who planted the man in the hollowed ground as a farmer plants a seed.

Vestiges of war

WAR

———— ⌘ ————

etween 1940 and 1976, while Don Alberto lived the dream he'd dreamed of coffee, El Salvador, the size of Massachusetts, was many countries in one. There was the sur face, and there was all that lay beneath the surface, the progress and also the retrogress, the stability as well as the antecedents of civil war. El Salvador was the geography of contradictions, crests, and fault lines. It would seethe for several decades before it blew.

The facts: Overthrown in 1944 by students, workers, and progressive military officers, El Brujo was gone, and in his absence the country was going modern—building new roads and power stations, new water purification plants, diversifying its agro-exports economy, attracting foreign cash, controlling the malaria and yellow fever that had, in combination with the poorness of the roadways, rendered El Salvador's lower coastlands economically useless for years. Coffee prices rose and coffee producers, financers, exporters took advantage of the profits, buying American things and European vacations, acquiring a taste for consumerism and boasting of the new inventions— new strains of coffee, new ways of picking, new uses of shade trees, new pesticides and drying equipment—they were trying out in the hills. Cities expanded to accommodate the sudden middle class, there was a swollen surge of students, there was the dawn of city unions, there was the claim, made in several quarters, that El Salvador provided proof of the power of capitalism, proof of the wisdom of John F. Kennedy's Alliance for Progress. There was advertising, endlessly, for the miracle of coffee, promotional campaigns directed at the new patron saints of the country of the Savior, those bold, those free, those enviably wealthy Americans.

"If you examine the medical and scientific writings about coffee," one Salvadoran Coffee Association pamphlet of that era boasts pompously, ridiculously,

> you will find a wealth of evidence that America's favorite beverage deserves its popularity. You will find, for instance, that coffee sharpens the analytical faculties of the mind. It increases the flow of ideas. It brightens the perception—sight, hearing, touch and other senses. It inspires reason and judgment and self control. But that is not all. Coffee increases physical strength, speed, and accuracy of movements. Yet the remarkable thing is this: the stimulating action of coffee does not leave behind any depression or fatigue. Its action is to assist the muscles in eliminating the poisons of fatigue. If a person who is tired drinks a cup of coffee, he begins to feel better right away. It does not, like a narcotic, simply dull the feeling of exhaustion. Rather, it steps up the physical output. . . . The greatest writers, poets, scholars have long been and are today great users of coffee. Where else in the world will you find a friend who gives so much and asks so little in return?

The wealthy, Robert Armstrong and Janet Shenk, iron-
ically observed,

> share a culture of genteel mediocrity, insulated from
> all but the most crass of twentieth-century con-
> sumerism. Their sons and daughters, sent to the
> United States for a college degree, rarely aspire
> beyond the expensive "party school," ending up in
> second-rate provincial colleges far from the main-
> stream of contemporary thought. The exceptions
> who study at Harvard or Yale must confront that
> mediocrity when they come back.
>
> Returning home, these young oligarchs can
> look forward to marriage, hopefully to a member of
> one of the "families" and, if a man, a place in one of
> the family businesses. If a woman, then there is the
> joy of babies and pampering by her husband and the
> servants. The periodic trip to Miami is the occasion
> for the revival of romance.
>
> There is the country house. There is the beach
> house. There is the city house in the San Benito or
> Escalón sections of San Salvador, the capital. The
> Mercedes is parked in the driveway; the strains of
> Montovani waft through the night air and the ice
> tinkles in the glass of imported scotch. . . .
>
> The rest of the country—the lazy, the drinker,
> the worthless, the "Indios"—they are there to make
> them money. And they are to stay in their place.

Also, therefore, these facts: Dispossession and privation continued to shadow the peasants who had made their homes on
strips of land that no true farmer wanted. So long as the lower

coastlands were plagued by water-borne diseases, so long as there were no roads to feed that region's progress, some had made their scrappy stands, braving the elements and farming the earth not on behalf of exports but for the sake of family survival.

Once cotton was established along the country's coast, however, once small land holdings were consolidated to make way for sugarcane, once coffee prices soared and further elevated the stature of coffee farming, peasants everywhere were systematically evicted. Adding insult to injury was the stifling lack of jobs, for cotton, sugarcane, and coffee offer only seasonal, low-paying employment, hardly enough to stake a family's living on, to buy an egg, to raise a pig, to buy medicine for diarrhea. For thousands upon thousands of the Salvadoran poor, suffering was the flip side of post–World War II advances. Progress meant nothing more than the fact that the last of the land wasn't theirs to share.

If city unions thrived, rural collectives and associations were illegal. If the ranks of teachers and doctors swelled, they did not swell in the hills, where illiteracy and malnutrition were every-day companions. If the country in general was flush with extra colones, it wasn't investing them in campesino craftwork or labor. Foreign investment might have soared, but so had the profits sponged out of the country. Even the 1965 implementation of a national minimum wage hurt the peasants more than it helped them, as large estate owners responded by reducing the number of those they hired, discriminating against women, whom they defined as "less productive," and eliminating the traditional daily tortilla from the wages. Often only Christmas brought relief, a week-long holiday in the midst of harvest season, when extra centavos went to plastic toys and *chicha,* to the fireworks that lit the New Year's sky until early in the morning. The peasant poor could play during the holy week of

Christmas, pull the lizards off the trees, spin the tops they might have whittled, listen to the songs of the kiskadees high in the trees.

But the truth remained: Like water up against a dam, the vast majority of the peasant poor had no place to go, no place to be, until the dam burst and some finally spilled across the border into Honduras, where banana growers needed pickers. Even exile wasn't sustainable. A four-day "soccer war" in the summer of 1969 pitted Honduras against El Salvador, left 3,000 dead and 6,000 injured and sent close to half the emigrants home—some 130,000 Salvadoran refugees who had nothing to do and no way to survive, save to join the crowded ranks of nearly idle vendors who on a good day sold a burlap bag or cotton blanket, or shined some shoes, or won the lottery, or found an afternoon's escape by tying a kite to a mezcal string and flying it high in a cemetery.

Reforms were talked about, sure. Vague packages put forth by concerned politicians that were met, as Salvadoran concern has so often been met, by noisy opposition, obfuscating alternatives. Still: three quarters of the population didn't have the money to buy what the new temples of industry were producing. Still: domestic food production was on the decline as fields of beans, maize, and rice gave way to sugarcane and coffee, as the population grew larger and hungrier. Still: being healthy was a privilege, having water was a privilege, babies were dying of dehydration, *babies were dying with their heads caved in from dehydration*, while their parents, brothers, sisters, aunts, uncles, grandparents were dying or wounded or malnourished, too, curing themselves or mostly not curing themselves with *guarumo* leaves and chicken fat, with iguana lard and fox turds, with jars of mysterious snake powder to press against their hurt.

National University students were taking notice, staging a

protest so radical in 1972 that the government felt forced to shut down the campus with tanks and planes. The Jesuit priests were taking notice, too, preaching self-determination in the hills. By the 1970s, with some 70 percent of the country's arable land in the hands of the top 10 percent of landowners, it had all become a kettle without a lid.

"Conditions within the country are said to be ripe for a revolution," David Browning observed in 1971. "With revolution it is claimed that a new socialist concept of the function of the land will provoke the changes necessary to solve the country's problems. Perhaps only violent change will provide sufficient impetus to overcome the present great inequalities of wealth, the widespread poverty, and the appalling lack of even the most basic medical and social services for the majority." Still, Browning noted, "communist leaders in El Salvador admit that the ease of movement through the country, the mobility of the army, and the ability of the government to check an incipient uprising in any part of the national territory means that a communist takeover remains a remote possibility."

Forty years after the murderous *matanza*, El Salvador was teetering on the edge of cataclysm. One could look the other way, but not for long. "Unions were organizing strikes, students were demonstrating, opposition political parties were actually winning elections, the Church was defending the rights of peasants to organize themselves, and all of these groups were demanding agrarian reform," observed the political scientist Liisa North in December of 1981. "For the oligarchy, the political opening had gone too far."

As the decade opened, El Salvador had its own army, its own national guard (to protect landowners from suspect peasants), its own national police (to protect against urban crimes), its own treasury police (to control borders, harbors, and airports), and its own paramilitary force, called ORDEN, a civilian enterprise that was designed to protect the country from communism and that achieved this goal by paying peasants to rat on peasants. All were known for their violent tactics. All were, for various reasons, feared. All were answered, in due course, by angry, driven-to-their-own-extremes guerrillas: the Popular Forces of Liberation–Farabundo Martí, the Popular Revolutionary Army, the Armed Forces of National Resistance, and the Revolutionary Party of Central American Workers.

The ideological battlefield had been drawn. Tensions escalated, and escalated once more. There was the blatant fraud that accompanied the 1972 presidential elections—the crowning of the Party of National Conciliation candidate Colonel Arturo Molina as leader despite the fact that José Napoleón Duarte, a moderate proponent of agrarian reform, had clearly won. There was the failed coup following that election, and the subsequent bloody eviction of Duarte from the country, and there was all that was happening in the hills—the students and the Jesuits supporting the peasants in their plight—teaching them to read, teaching them to organize, risking reprisals, fighting the reprisals that came. Arms filtered in from Nicaragua and Cuba. Strikes flared up and kidnappings terrified the rich as peasant forces sought to finance operations by ransoming wealthy Salvadorans.

And in the summer of 1975, while Don Alberto still worked his coffee lands without suspicion of his cancer, while parts of the country still entertained the illusion that tempers would somehow settle without apocalyptic bloodshed, my husband watched as police opened fire on thousands of peacefully protesting students. Bill had just arrived at a high school campus above San Salvador, where he was scheduled to play a game of volleyball. He was headed for the gym when he heard what he thought was the backfire of a car. Like the backfire of a car, he says, but much too regular, too loud, too much like machine-gun fire, which, of course, it was. The peaceful protest became a terrified stampede. Bullets flew and the protesters scattered, the protesters ran, the protesters were jumping: flinging themselves off a concrete overpass into the oncoming traffic below. Thirty-seven would die or disappear that day. My husband would not forget it. Later I ask him if he knew why it had happened. If he knew why the students had marched, and then why the police had thought to shoot them.

"No," he says, thinking quietly. "I don't remember if I ever actually knew why it started."

"Think about it," I say. "Think about 1975. What was the big event?"

"Hosting the Miss Universe pageant," he says, after a moment's reflection, though I can tell he doesn't think there is a conceivable connection.

"Yeah. Right. 1975. Miss Universe comes to El Salvador."

"I guess so," he says. Nothing more.

"Thirty-seven people gone," I press. "Thirty-seven people gone because they dared to protest that their country had spent one million dollars to host a beauty pageant. While half the children in your country were starving. And most of the parents couldn't read."

There was no not having an opinion anymore. There was no not choosing sides.

It was within this whorl of ever-deepening antagonism that Bill's father, Mario, took on the fifty *manzanas* of St. Anthony's Farm and tried to make things grow. Farming hardly suited him; it wasn't land he'd grown to love. He was the American-born son of two Philippine parents. He liked theater. He liked the arts. He liked to read. When he fell in love with Nora when they were both studying in San Francisco, he was young, too young to understand that giving his heart to her meant moving to her country, meant living what would be her life and therefore not his own. He was a student in a Jesuit college when they met. She was a student in the women's college across the way, taking an American education like all her siblings. Both of them were physically beautiful people; they made a gorgeous couple. In St. Carmen's Church, where my husband would one day surrender his first confession, they became husband and wife.

"He liked riding horses," Bill says now, trying to imagine what it was like for his father those first years. "And he made his own friends, other Americans who'd moved down there." And there were the jobs that he took on with varying degrees of pleasure—a management stint at the local Colgate division, a job managing the manufacturing arm of a local furniture venture, a novel job of selling properties under the aegis of El Salvador's first-ever real estate firm. He did his work. He made his friends. He played polo at the club. He answered his wife's rapid, dramatic Spanish with his own sanguine English and addressed his children in the language he'd grown up speaking.

And in 1976, after Don Alberto died, Mario took on the land his wife had been willed—took it on just as the tempers of his country were near to boiling. Bill was there with his father that first season, waiting out the lost semester, taking on odd jobs, selling stereos for a while in a local department store until the farm started needing him full-time. He would do whatever he could do, whatever could be done by one who doesn't know the growing secrets of a farm. He'd take the jeep down the road to the city and load up on fertilizer. He'd stand with his father and do payroll. He'd whistle for the horse they let roam free by the river, and when she made it up the hill, he'd climb on her back and go all around to make sure that the pickers were working the trees they'd been assigned.

But running a farm requires knowing what to look for. It takes practice, patience, a well-developed intuition. Running a farm means knowing, the way you know your own pulse, your own dreams, when to cut down the mature trees, where to install the tenderlings, how lush to let the shade trees grow, where to fertilize, how to get rid of the pests, whom to hire, whom to trust. In Don Alberto's absence, Bill's father chose the wrong man to trust, a campesino named Cupertino. He gave him leeway, and Cupertino took advantage, ignoring the weeds and assembling the wrong band of coffee pickers, favoring friends over productivity.

Cupertino let my father-in-law down. And besides, it was a bad time for coffee farming.

*R*epression and violence, kidnappings, strife had become the daily screed. A few months after Don Alberto passed away, General Carlos Humberto Romero, a conservative functionary of the right, bullied his way into power through an election so fraudulent that thousands of dead men were said to have cast votes. Protesters called for new elections, crowding San Salvador's Plaza Libertad to make their displeasure known, orating on stump boxes, buying tortillas from the vendors who'd gathered near to feed the crowds, churning up what at least one thought to call a "carnival" atmosphere. By February 28, 1977, some sixty thousand had gathered in the plaza, and the army, no longer tolerant, gave the throngs ten minutes to disperse. Upon hearing the command, the crowds broke into one loud song— voice over voice, verve over passion, they sang the national anthem. There were no second warnings. Bullets cut the protesters down, and when the crowds understood that there was murder in the air, they began to scream and run. Those who sought refuge in the nearest cathedral were pursued and, in cold Catholic blood, shot dead.

Two weeks later, on the twelfth of March, Father Rutilio Grande, a Jesuit priest who had gone up into the sugarcane region near Aguilares in August of 1972 to help the peasants find their voice, demand their rights, and build a better future, died along a country road at an assassin's hand. Two months afterwards, in May, one Father Alfonso Navarro would meet a brutal death as well, an act of "retaliation" for the kidnap and murder of a wealthy man. The church, long a defender and protector of the right, seemed to have swayed the other way, become an enemy of the oligarchs. Seeking at first to maintain a neutral stance, the new archbishop, Oscar Arnulfo Romero, pleaded with the government to investigate the murders of his friends. But when the government refused, when the crimes against the peasants continued mounting, Romero assumed a more progressive, outspoken role, sermonizing to the country over broadcast radio, calling for the end of army violence, the end of human rights abuses, the honoring of the commandments that were set out in the Bible.

But the words of no one, not even God, were heeded, and on November 24, 1977, General Romero created a state of emergency, suspended constitutional liberties, and gave his military an outright license to kill. Foreign investment withered. The economy was paralyzed. El Salvador, the fourth-largest producer of coffee in the world, was about to lose the power, stature, comforts that her crops—for good, for bad—had brought her.

Imagine Bill's father, then, set up against all this. Imagine this man who had named his eldest son for a character in an

American novel, who had studied business in college, who was not known for loving the feel of earth or the smell of gardens, taking it all suddenly on and faced with so many decisions. He trusted Cupertino, but Cupertino shouldn't have been trusted. He tried to do what Don Alberto would have done, but Don Alberto had not grown coffee in a war.

On October 15, 1979, General Romero was deposed in a coup by a cadre of army officers. He was replaced by a civilian-military junta, the country's last best hope against an all-out war. But the junta's best intentions failed—its desire to initiate land reforms, to conduct democratic elections, to even open the political process to the splintered guerrilla factions was thwarted by the military's lust for power. Even as junta talks were under way, paramilitary attacks on peasants continued, and it wasn't long before the civilian members of the junta stepped down, unwilling to participate in such a mockery of government. Other civilians filled their shoes. Reforms were promised. Reforms failed. The people grew more desperate. On January 22, 1980, some 220,000 gathered in the streets of San Salvador to protest against their country. Death squads, disappearances, murders: the protesters called for an end to all that, called for it, all witnesses tend to agree, with a certain peacefulness. But from above the Presidential Palace shots rang out, and dozens were killed, and dozens were trampled as the frightened throngs ran, screaming.

March 23: Archbishop Romero addresses his weekly broadcast directly to the country's soldiers: *I issue a special entreaty to the army, the national guard, police and military,* his voice rang out to some 75 percent of the Salvadoran people over radio from a station that the rightists had tried to bomb. *Do not kill your fellow peasants, your brothers and sisters. No soldier is obliged to obey an order which is against the law of God.* But the next day the archbishop would be silenced, too, killed by a single bullet shot through his heart as he stood giving mass in the Divine Providence Cancer Hospital. The 100,000 who thronged to his funeral left more than their tears; some left their blood. Once again the army snipers had gathered at their posts atop the palace. Once again the snipers let loose and fired, murdering the dozens of those who fell within the bullets' paths.

Soon two thousand would be dying every month. Soon five separate guerrilla groups would pool their anger and momentum and unite under a single banner, the Farabundo Martí National Liberation Front. Soon four American churchwomen traveling to El Salvador to work with victims of the war would disappear along the airport road and then be found: raped, shot, burnt, discarded. This was the first I'd ever heard of my husband's country. Or the first story I'd paid attention to. The first impression I held on to, then, for years. Four American women, church women. Raped. Shot. Burnt. Discarded. I was twenty when I read the news. El Salvador, I thought to myself. So this is El Salvador.

*W*ho could run a coffee farm in a country going crazy? Who could forge ahead, who could plan with discipline, in a place where nothing certain ruled, where corpses without faces, without limbs, with scattered hands, with torn-up genitals were rumored of and sometimes found? My husband's family owned land; they believed, like others who owned the land, that export agriculture was their nation's saving grace. That when the earth yielded, the whole country profited. That in order for the earth to yield, one had to protect the sprawling farms. Fracture a farm and the land grows inefficient, finances fail, the pickers' work grows piecemeal—that's what they believed. Fracture a farm and there'll be little to export, no colones to distribute, no way to keep the country from falling to its knees. Members of the coffee elite saw themselves as leaders of their country's progress, the way-pavers of economic growth and technological advance, of higher living standards.

In the spring of 1980, while the country's north and east were beset by sporadic, brutal fighting, while the capital hosted scenes of occasional pandemonium and bloodshed, while discontent brooded and festered in the coffee-saturated west, coffee growers throughout the nation were beset with new decrees. The seizure and redistribution of estates larger than five hundred hectares was being called for by reform-minded moderates. So was the nationalization of the banks and the nationalization of coffee exports. American Ambassador Robert White was dispatched to seek "a new model for profound . . . economic and social change." Nothing was reliable, nothing safe. There were murders in the hills, there were priests inciting conflict, the government had taken on the price management of coffee. Across the nation, the work on *fincas* stalled. Fertilizing, weeding, pruning, the planting of tenderlings—all was abandoned. It would take ten to twenty years for the plantations to recover.

In the wake of it all, there was a spate of odd inventions. Farmers who took up raising geese, hoping to produce paté and profits. Landowners who went to the sea and constructed hatcheries for shrimp. Bill's father, for his part, forsook the coffee for bamboo, replanting an entire side of St. Anthony's Farm with a plant that grows like weed.

"Bamboo," I ask. "Why bamboo?"

"For furniture," Bill answers. "For sale, to manufacturers."

"Did it work?"

"No, it didn't work."

"What happened?"

"St. Anthony's lost a lot of trees. And no one bought bamboo."

In 1984, one year after I met the man I'd marry, one year before I said *I do*, the revolutionary forces brought their war, in force, to the land Bill had grown up loving. They hid up in the hills and they attacked Santa Tecla's lifelines—her roads, her bridges, her buses, her dams, her electric generators and power lines. They fought back against the U.S.-supported army, the U.S. jets strafing their country. Meanwhile, the bamboo wasn't making money and the coffee was lying fallow, and Bill's father was mourning the loss of his best friend.

"Who was it?" I ask.

"Carlos Alfaro," Bill says. "The university president."

"What happened?"

"They blocked him in."

"What do you mean?"

"I mean that it was broad daylight and he was being driven to the campus, his driver up in front and his two body guards beside him." At the gates of the university, Bill says, they stopped where it was routine to stop, but then one truck pulled in front of them while another pulled behind. There was no out. Alfaro's car was locked in. The four men sat there helpless while the revolutionaries opened fire. Bullets through metal through flesh, and there was nothing left of Alfaro or his men.

In the summer of 1984 El Salvador was deep inside its war, and I was deep within my romance. The man I was going to marry told me stories of his country, and the headlines told me other stories, and there was no correspondence. Bill came from land, from the landed's side of war, and yet he came from a family that had always loved the purported enemy. Lenora and Juan, Tiburcio and Lydia, Nicha and Tomas, María López and her drunken Santana, the community of St. Anthony's Farm. They had been housed, fed, confirmed, married, priested, feted, trusted, and not out of pity but out of respect, not out of charity but because there would have been no farm without them, there would have been no coffee on the trees. I wanted to know what Don Alberto would have done had he survived through the heat of the war. I wanted to know who Bill would have been had he not come to the States, to Philadelphia, where I was.

But there is no knowing most things; there is only the sitting close and listening, only the imagining later on. If I'd met Bill in El Salvador, would we be lovers, or would we be bitter enemies? If I'd married him in America, would we remain in two separate worlds? I chose to believe that in time we'd grow less strangely, that his tales would become less astonishing, that my tales would become somehow alluring, that politics could be overcome, that we would fill each other's vacant spaces. But then one afternoon that summer, Bill found a letter in his box, his name and address written carefully out with the impeccable handwriting of his father. A sign. A warning. "What is it?" I asked. "What is the news?" *Your mother and I are parting ways. Your mother and I are parting.* The same message Bill would receive from his mother a few days on, in Spanish.

*T*he first time I went to El Salvador it was 1986. I looked for the war; I found Tiburcio in Nora's garden. I looked for fear; I found only my own: fear of the roads, fear of the dogs, fear of my husband's Spanish. I had little appreciation then for who Bill's mother was, what she was up against, this divorcée whacking bamboo loose from a coffee farm, this woman, her sons and husband gone, loving the land her father left her. St. Anthony's

Farm was Don Alberto's farm in the stories Bill had told. It took a while for me to understand that it was now a daughter's stronghold.

Without my noticing at first, and for a long time, Nora was learning the farm, learning how to make things grow, listening to the people who could make tenderlings from seeds, tapping into the good will that her father had left her, along with the deed, going about her business with a pragmatic sense of humor. Nora had been an entrepreneur all her life—raising watermelons with a friend and pocketing profits, running pricey clothes from Miami to the Salvadoran hoi polloi—and she was famous for her efficiency, her unromantic take on trouble. *What needs to be done?* She could ask the question and not be overwhelmed by the multitudinous answers. She could plot it out, bit by bit: yank the bamboo, recarve the terrace, plant the tenderlings, prune the trees. *We need fertilizer, so I will go myself into the city and bring it back, and also, I have decided to plant more* pepeto *trees because they close their leaves at night and let in the dew before they open them again at sunrise to forestall evaporation; that's what my workers told me.* She whistled and the horse came hoofing from the river; she mounted and went up and down the hills. She hired men who could be trusted. She assumed the risks that are a coffee grower's fate—borrowing working capital to finance the weeding and replantings, to pay the workers for paltry harvests, to cover the costs of waiting, waiting for the coffee to get sold, to start again.

The war took its course, Nora took hers. The second time I visited El Salvador, May 1988, I looked for fear and found it. I sat at parties and passed *escabeche*, listened all the while to the bombs detonating in the hills, to the helicopters prowling, and the tinkle of plates, and the irrelevant, irreverent laughter. I went to the house of a ransomed man and listened to him talk about

the kidnapping. I watched the nights go dark while the generators blew, saw the soldiers—armed and erect—along the highways, inside the marketplaces, in the restaurants, outside the gift
shops where Adela and I one day went shopping for souvenirs
for home. *Ay, Beth, this is beautiful, see? Ay, Beth, buy this basket for
your mother, buy this paper for yourself.* I went to the orphanage
with Nora, the Patronato Hogar Adalberto Guirola of Santa
Tecla, where white was the color—white pillars, white tiles,
white sleeves, white light, white like a symbol or a sign—until I
went inside and saw where the children sleep, saw a long room
full of cots with yellow blankets, cots without pillows, without
dolls or toys, and then a second room, another crowded room,
where red predominated: red covers, red bedposts, red paper
posters on the wall. In the orphanage I saw children who had
each been assigned a friend, a hand to hold, a companion to help
keep the parentlessness at bay, though the gruesome fact was
that some sixty thousand children were already orphaned by the
war. In San Rafael, the hospital for the poor, where I also went
because Nora wanted me to see, because Nora volunteered
there as she volunteered at the orphanage, there was compan-
ionship, too—women sharing gurneys, women sharing beds
among nurses in pink uniforms, and above it all, a dragonfly
knocking its celestial wings against the clerestory glass.

That week the U.S. embassy would be tested by the fire of
guerrillas. Within a year, the promise of a cease-fire would be
shattered, voters would be executed, new offenses would be
launched in the neighborhood where Bill's father lived. In
October 1989, new attempts at peace were destroyed when a
bomb blasted through the Salvadoran Workers National Union
Federation headquarters, killing ten and wounding twenty-nine.
In 1990, peace again grew elusive when proposed reforms drew

the ire of the right. Coffee harvests were lower than they'd been for thirty years. Salvadorans who could find a way emigrated to the States and sent their paychecks home.

Through all of this, Nora kept giving time to the orphans and the sick in the city, kept farming the green hills up above. She grew to love her country even more under impossible circumstances, grew that much more impassioned about the community of growers, pickers, singers, cooks that Don Alberto had housed and celebrated—respecting their wisdom on tortillas and picking, bringing them doctors, new shoes, fiestas, a priest, risking herself, at times, to get their babies baptized. Because if coffee was in many ways implicated in a complicated civil war, if coffee pitted the landed against the landless in horrid, brutal fashion, it didn't have to, it didn't always, it wasn't like that at St. Anthony's Farm. Nora concluded, as Don Alberto, the revolutionary cum gardener before her had concluded, that in a country whose fortunes are tied to crops what could be made right would be made right in her own community of coffee growers, among families who had lived and worked together for forty years. They together would make the coffee grow, help preserve a small fraction of a vastly deforested country, provide a refuge for the peculiar, strange, and thrilling things that had marched north and lumbered south and then mingled on the land bridge. The shade tree canopies that protect coffee from rain, sun, wind, protect the atmosphere as well, protect the valley lands from flooding, extend a home to subtropical grasses, tropical fruits, medicinal plants, orchids, bougainvillea, 120 migrating birds, beetles, ants, wasps, spiders, possums, squirrels, snakes, raccoons, anteaters, kinkajous, gray foxes, gophers, iguanas, sac-winged bats and whiskered bats and fringe-lipped bats and leaf-chin bats and mice, there are so many mice, and maybe, if you're lucky, a spider monkey, a lone coyote, a nervous puma, an ocelot, the rare crested eagle, the rarer-yet jaguar, and, if you look hard enough, some seventeen species of hummingbirds, so many sudden blurs of color, so many mysteries among trees. If coffee betrays a country into conflict, if coffee *becomes*, in so many ways, the politics of a country which cannot survive without its crops, it also stands loyal to the earth. Those who own the land where it grows are the privileged and the burdened.

La Barra de Santiago

SPANISH

When the Salvadorans speak, I see a flock of birds. Starlings or crows, it doesn't matter: just birds gnashing, pitching, thwacking, heaving, flapping like some oriflamme strung out on a breeze. I listen, but I see instead, stalking the Spanish with my mind's eye, urging the flock to divide, the throng to dissipate, the birds to wheel off as single, appreciable words. One word on a wing, another word, and air to spare between: I watch for this. I wait to take a photograph. But the Spanish gangs upon itself, coagulates, and masses—the *rr*'s somersaulting into the *e*'s, the *h*'s muting themselves, the syllables cleaving to one another's breasts. Only occasionally is there the flash of the familiar: *muy bien, no tengo, me llamo, mucho gusto, por favor, hola, sí.* Only occasionally do I reach out and make my snatch at understanding, steal a frozen frame. Mostly I am daunted by the Hitchcockian spectacle of so many birds, by the sounds that I see when I am listening.

Three times I have bought myself manuals and tapes, self-help Spanish. Three times I've sat in private places, playing mimic with the instructors.

Como te llamas?
Me llamo Beth.
Como dice?

Me llamo Beth.

Puede repetir, por favor?

Me llamo Beth. Soy de América. Habla usted inglés?

It's a game of charades: *Sounds like:* a ripple, a flattening, a stutter, a smack. *Looks like:* a gaggle of indivisible birds. *What is it?* Beth's Spanish. It's an exercise that teaches me more about myself than it will ever teach me about Spanish. I fear, I've learned, the freewheeling acrobatics of sound. I fear the smudges between consonants and the inbred variables of vowels. I fear the mistakes I will make, the infantalizing of my speech, the helplessness that is invoked, at last, by the formal *usted* and the informal *tu,* by the regular and irregular verbs, by the *v*'s that are made to sound like *b*'s, by that damned rolling *r,* which I will never, in this lifetime, approximate. I need words on paper, the cushioning *ahh* of white space, the time to remember the rules, the privilege of knowing what's been said. Words are only symbols. I need to see them, after all.

Now this winter, with Jeremy at school and Bill at work, and a trip to El Salvador looming, I try again. The noisiest thing in my house is the amaryllis, which has stalked up obediently all December long and finally, this week, parted its beak, revealing a fabulous mutancy of striped color. It sits in a window against a backdrop of snow, its pollen-encrusted anthers upturned like so many beseeching hands, some petals stuck to some petals in the sticky aftermath of birth. Two of the blooms are as big as faces, as finely molded as trumpets. I turn the grandest one toward me and, a book on my lap, a cassette in the machine, get to work. I feel like Eliza Doolittle at Henry Higgins's desk, testing out my vowels, forcing myself upon the hapless double *r*'s. Too soon, with lavish cruelty, the lesson gets away from me— swoops from a civilized *hola* to a complicated marketplace transaction in a matter of minutes. I rewind the tape. Again, there is that *hola*. I like *hola*. I can do *hola*. But it's a precipitous slope and soon I'm sliding once more through familiar complications toward the overstocked marketplace. Damn the marketplace. I go back to *hola*, and I am greeted as a friend. *Hola*, the tape says. *Hola*, I say back.

Bill calls. I answer. "What are you up to?" he wants to know.

"Trying to put spaces around your Spanish words," I say. If a voice could roll its eyes, then mine just did.

"Really?" Bill says.

"Really what?" My voice goes docile like a dog lowering its head in anticipation of a loving nudge, a sweep of encouragement, a *good girl* endearment for my culture-bridging endeavors.

"I mean," Bill clarifies, "*really* you can't just tell where one word ends and another begins?"

"No, actually, I find that just slightly troublesome," I say, my head snapped back upright, my faux smile at the ready, though there's no one here to see it. "Your Spanish is all pitches and slides and rat-a-tat-tats. It doesn't know where its own lousy syllables stop and begin." I blame it on Bill, this Spanish, whenever I can. It feels like a more defensible position.

"Huh," Bill says, refusing my invitation to an old battle.

"Huh what?" I want to know. "Come on," I say, "when you go to France, do you know what the French people are saying."

"No," Bill says.

"See?"

"But I know where the words begin and end." Bill doesn't say this to one-up me. He's honestly and sincerely baffled that his wife of so many years still can't make heads or tails of his first language.

"Look, Bill, I'm trying to learn this. I've been sitting here all morning talking to the amaryllis as if it were some kind of ear trumpet."

"Maybe you need some different kinds of tapes," he says, after a pause, trying to be helpful.

"Maybe," I say. "Though this is my third set. And I hate this one the most."

"Why?"

"Because it claims a 100 percent success rate. Claims to make Spanish *easy*. Can you believe that? The nerve."

"Okay," Bill says; he's still perplexed. "Well. Look. I've got a deadline. I've got to go. I'm sure something has sunk in by now. Some little fraction of Spanish, something. Just keep trying. Stick with it. Something's bound to click." What he doesn't say, what he doesn't offer, is, *Hey, Beth, don't worry. I'll teach you.* He tried teaching me the guitar once and that was enough. What possible good could my lisping at him in his native, happy tongue do our marriage? What aggravation and fatal reassessments would it provoke? I must go my own way with this, and this we both know. Bill stops short of the offer. I stop short of the request.

*I*t's from the language doctors that I draw my comforts, my bevy of psycho-lingual excuses. Think, these doctors write in their many textbooks, of all that must happen in the brain for a language to get learned. A physically continuous signal must be divvied into categories; a wash of sound must be heard in fragments as phonemes. Subsequently, miraculously, these phonemes must be linked up with their meanings and, at the same time, accents, rhythms, intonations, and all related tricks and trills must be trusted with their intents. This is easy, you say. Babies do it every day. They fight their way through the rushing, chiming, clanging, overwhelming blare of sound to a place of familiarity and calm. By the time they're five or six months old, their brains are encoded with the contrasts and syllabic structures of their particular linguistic environments. Their brains are *engrammed*. Their capacity to hear everything diminishes. Their ability to understand what is being specifically said to and all around them sprouts a pedicel and blooms; their brains reorganize around this powerful, incipient knowledge. Babies' learning circuitry is plastic and avid. Babies are pioneers. Babies are brilliant.

"Everyone knows that it is much more difficult to learn a second language in adulthood than a first language in childhood," Steven Pinker writes, to console second-language stymied fools like me. Because even if you get it right in vocabulary, you have to master the phonology, the underlying grammar that girds the sound patterns of each language. Up until the age of six, language development in so-called normal children is a veritable guarantee. After the age of thirteen, the brain begins its decline, loses neurons, slows its metabolism, all of which makes second-language acquisition harder and harder.

This is not to say that I shouldn't feel some shame at my inability to go native with my husband. My friend Susan taught herself Italian in a year, then took her writing students to Rome. My friend Vicki did French in high school and switched to Spanish in college with few apparent problems, she says, modestly, as Vicki does. My husband's brother Mario speaks impeccable Spanish, English, Italian, French, and one summer, just for kicks, he taught himself sign language. Bill's youngest brother, Rodi, converses in Japanese. And my friend Alane, you should see what she has done: translated a story from Italian into English just because she longed to share it with a friend.

And then there's Jeremy, who rescues me and the amaryllis

when he comes home from school at last. "Whatcha been doing, Mom?" he asks, when he walks in upon a family room strewn with cassettes and paperbacks.

"I've been listening to something," I say. "Here. Sit down. Listen with me."

He grabs an Orangina first, knocks off the cap, slouches down in the love seat, cocks his chin in my direction, half closes his eyes to concentrate. "I'm ready."

"Okay," I say, sticking in the first cassette. "Tell me honestly what you make of this." Perfect, proper Spanish conversation ensues, a flock of birds goes wheeling across the backdrop of my imaginary sky. I half close my eyes too, hoping that this will bring me strength. I wait ten minutes, then snap off the tape. "What did you think?" I ask Jeremy. "A bunch of hogwash?"

"Well, Mom," Jeremy says, taking a swig of Orangina before he speaks. "It's like this. First they were talking about where they came from. Then they were talking about numbers. Then they went to some marketplace and they changed some money and they bought bananas."

"Well thanks a lot," I say.

"What?" he says, genuinely innocent.

"Just," I pass my hand in front of my face like some postprime diva. "Just. Look, Jer. Just . . . go do your own thing, will you? Go play. Do whatever. Have yourself a ball."

"What did I do?"

"Nothing."

"What's wrong?"

"Nothing."

"You asked me what I thought!"

"I did. That's right. And you're a very smart kid."

"I take Spanish in school, Mom." He shrugs. "It's easy. For

me. And besides, I only understand a little. I don't understand the whole thing, like Dad."

"This I know," I say. "And I'm proud of you. Now give me a kiss, okay? And go play."

Minutes later, the telephone rings. I've got the tape back in, but I'm only half listening, half engaged, more than half defeated, still shaking my head, bemused, at Jeremy's natural proficiency at a language that still is garble to me. He is his father's son, after all.

"What are you doing?" Bill wants to know after our hellos.

"I'm listening to your Spanish people jabber," I say morosely.

"Has it gotten any better?"

"What?"

"The Spanish?"

"It's pretty much the same as it always was."

"Well. Just keep trying. It will come."

"I am. I doubt it."

"How's Jeremy?"

"He's great. He's always great. He knows your Spanish."

"I know."

"Yeah. I know, too. He's pretty amazing." A pause. Then: "Bill?"

"Yes?"

"I want to learn this. I want to learn Spanish for real this time."

"Well then you will, Beth, you will. Just keep trying."

"I don't know if trying is enough. I think my brain is clogged. Fatally. Anyway, what are you up to?"

"I have a deadline."

"You should get back to work, okay?"

"Tell Jeremy hi from me."

"I will. We'll see you later. Don't work too hard."

I hang up and stop the tape, start picking up around the room. The amaryllis watches my every move. The sun has fallen outside; the snow on the deck beyond the window seems whiter than the sky. In a few minutes I'll go upstairs and play a game with Jeremy; I'll tell him how proud I am of all he knows, of his affinity for his father's Spanish. For now, in this interlude, I turn to the computer, to electronic mail; I turn to help. *Adela,* I write. *I'm having trouble learning Spanish. I try and try, but I'm lousy. How in the world did you ever learn your English? Do you think there is any hope for me?* I write to Adela because I trust Adela. Because she lived in the States longer than her sisters, a student first, and then a glamorous military wife.

I sit in silence. Within moments a message is returned, as if Adela has just been hovering there somewhere in sunny Santa Tecla, El Salvador, picking up around her own rooms, waiting for my question. *Hola Beth,* she starts out, like the girlfriend and confidante she has become, the reassuring bridge back to her country. *At the beginning it will be hard,* she writes, *but Spanish its easier than English, and also you should have William practice it with you.* A break in the electronic lines ensues, as if she's been thinking, and then:

You know, English was very hard to learn, as it is written one way and pronounce another way, and the other thing I did wrong I was translating every word, until a nun told me not to translate, she told me I had to think in English, and I thought she was a nut, there is not one way I can think in English.

I can practically hear Adela say this, hear her: breathless.

But I finally did, she concludes.

And you take care.

Love.

Two chairs at the farm

BEANS

⸺◦⊶⊷◦⸺

*I*t is Bill's idea to go to El Salvador to welcome the coming of the new millennium. I have my doubts. There's the Y2K no-computers-no-airplanes-no-banks-no-refrigerators threat hanging over the planet's head, and then there's all the news that escapes from El Salvador itself—the escalation of crime, the escalation of *violent* crime, the recent nasty assault of an American woman. Besides, it seems odd to spend New Year's Eve in a country that's been tossing off explosives with purposeful vengeance for years. But Bill feels strongly about being home when all those zeros turn, and I feel strongly about not being so afraid, and so we pack our summer things in winter and head off for the airport. The air is turbulent as we fly from Philadelphia to Atlanta, worse as we fight the clouds between Atlanta and Cuzcatlán International. When at last we hit the tarmac with a jolt, we're thrown back cruelly against the cushions of our seats. I reach across Bill to hold Jeremy's hand. Bill touches my cheek with his finger. The brakes win their battle against the jet plane's reckless speed, but not before a calamitous nausea wins its battle with me.

At last, buckled into the seats of Nora's jeep, we swallow the dust and spits of gravel that the open windows hurl in like insults. Bloated-bellied cattle are grazing in the highway median strips as they always do, and an overloaded sugarcane truck is jackknifed off to the side, the brown sticks it couldn't handle toppled to the asphalt. The closer we get to the city, the more crowded the median strips grow, not just with famished cows but with metal shacks and smoking *comales*, with lines of laundry, cardboard boxes, entire communities of homeless. Off to the side of the highway, on the low skirts of some hills, the land is carved out, treeless, a somber dirty color, home to so many concrete condos stacked up like a child's blocks. They look abandoned, post-apocalyptic, fatally devoid of flowers, though in fact they are brand-new and an answer to some prayers, an object of envy to those making tortilla paste in the crowded median strips. El Salvador is thirsty, it occurs to me, and its dust nicks my face as it hurtles.

In the car Bill and his mother talk up front—gossip, I understand it to be, updates on old friends. A half hour in, she turns to me and says in her difficult English, "I'd take that gold heart from my neck." Confused, still dazed from the fit of nausea on the plane, I lean across Jeremy and ask her to repeat herself. Her accent thick and impatient, she says, "Also. Remove the bracelets. Also. Take off your watch. And if you care about your wedding rings, you will not wear them here." In her car, in her country, I heed her caution, I obey. I feel naked and strange, my right hand unstitched from its wrist, the fingers on my left hand poorly fit together, my neck, which I keep stroking, a sudden virgin canvas. I have never been asked to remove my jewelry before, and here I am, fifteen years in, wanting nothing new to fear.

After unbelievable tie-ups and traffic, and more than one gassed-up dead cow on the road, we arrive at Nora's house in Santa Tecla. Turning again from the conversation she long ago resumed with Bill, she tells me that the man with the Uzi—the man in the guardhouse, right there, the one saluting—is paid to guard her, that he is getting an extra turkey dinner so that he'll remember to keep us safe as well. "Don't go any further than where he can see you," she says. "And if you must take photographs, hold your camera to your chest. Don't yield. And trust no one but family. And, as always, don't drink the water." Jeremy looks at me. I look at him. We heft our luggage into the house, allow a massive iron door to close shut behind us.

Inside we are met by a little girl whose name is music: Ana Gabriela. Her mother's gone missing, we're told, and sometimes she lives here in this house, just like the granddaughter Nora always wanted, though in fact, she is Ana Ruth's granddaughter. She is seven and what else but dark haired, and her shy smile just barely reveals the row of new teeth that are coming in uneven. Up and down the cool tile floors of Nora's house she slides, sometimes with a Barbie in her hand and sometimes with the silks of corn husks slipping through her fingers, evidence of the work she has been doing with the maids. Soon enough a party has collected: familiar welcoming faces, familiar gestures. Nora's sisters. Nora's friends. Rafael, now a dentist down the street. Tiburcio, making himself useful in Nora's still-immaculate garden. There is chutney on crackers and gin for the grown-ups and Coke without ice, the only thing Jeremy for the next eight days will be allowed to drink. And the talk lazy Susans around, and I am easy with it as it comes and it goes. And sometimes, all of the sudden, there are quick bright breaks of English or entire sentences in Spanish which I take on, I understand. The stories come from Adela, mostly, who sits, like a best girlfriend, at my side, and from Nora, who smiles and laughs and serves and nods for emphasis.

"You know, Beth. Our friends across the street? Robbed. Thirty-five paintings gone."

"You know, Beth, two weeks ago and one block down, they tied the maid and the gardener to their chairs and hauled away what they could carry, and then came back for more."

"You know, Beth, they steal the saints from the church."

"You know, Beth. I was going to a party. I was knocking on a door. And all of the sudden they put a gun against my head."

"No, Adela. No," I say. "Impossible."

"Not impossible. It happened to me."

I get that funny feeling in my fingers, my hand. I cannot find the heart around my neck.

In the kitchen, Nicha is steaming tamales in their banana-leaf wraps. In the garden, Tiburcio hangs like a shadow over cow's tongue and a lemon tree, among ficus and green-white-yellow fertile things that I cannot name still. From hand to hand move the family's latest photographs, and then a book of faded black-and-whites, and then stories—stories I have heard so many times now that I know them, in English or in Spanish. And now a bottle of wine goes around, accompanied by the vodka, and there is more chutney, and Jeremy decides to fill up with another Coke.

"You know, at night," I hear the maids say. "I think I hear the oxcart coming, and then I think it is the old witch, Siguanaba, with her candles made of bone."

"You know Cupertino?" Now Adela. "He'd become a good man, an honest worker. And then they found him swinging from a shade tree, strung upside down by his own safety rope, stung to death by wasps."

It goes on: The same stories. The new stories. The filter of Spanish. My husband far away, and Jeremy contented with his Coke. After a while, I retreat to the front of the house, unlock the door and peer through the iron grate at the street in Santa Tecla. Every house barricaded in. Every wall and roof crowned with concertina wire. The sidewalks barren save for the stray coconut tree; the skies excruciatingly blue, except for the *clarinero* bird that sits undaunted on the wire, between the razors. In places I see how the bougainvillea and the luscious San Carlos won't be contained—how they thrust themselves through the grates and the barbs and all the things that are not safe upon this street, that seem less safe since our last visit. I feel a hand against my hand. It is the little motherless girl, Ana Gabriela, stolen in beside me, like a shadow. I close her sweet corn silky hand in mine and bend down to her height. She giggles, showing me all her teeth, and then she points outside. I answer her, "*Sí, Ana Gabriela. Sí.*" Again she giggles, knowing it's almost all I can say, knowing that we'll find other ways to talk.

A few days later, we decide to go east, toward cities that Bill himself hasn't seen for thirty years. The roads, of course, are impossible—the width of one lane turned into two, then divided by impatience and bad manners into three, so that it is all a game of chicken, everything hurtling toward everything else only to duck, at the last moment, into safety. Beside me in the back seat, Nora notices that I have returned the diamond to my marriage finger. "Swallow it," she says, half joking. "That way you will know that it's still yours."

It takes two hours of mostly bad roads and worse congestion to reach San Vicente. Here again the houses look like walls, windows don't exist, and the barbed wire tangles with the birds, the greens, the lavishly beautiful baskets of radishes and onions. On a side street we find the door Nora has brought us all this way for, and pushing through we enter not a house but a courtyard—roosters, weeds open to the sky. In the very back, under the cover of a collapsing corrugated metal roof, stands the candy maker, Argelia, her thin, loose hair the color of the steam behind her, her hands rolling out snakes of something sticky, black. With a pair of scissors, she snips the snake into tiny pieces and lays them, so many black eyes, to her side. Beside her a girl, no more than ten, lifts milk out of a cauldron with a paddle and turns it over and over and over again, the paddle taller than the girl, the steaming milk like a bolt of ivory fabric. At my feet, the roosters have begun a game of soccer with a ball that they discovered in the weeds. In a broken wire cage hanging from a stumpy tree limb, a parrot flashes the riot of feathers on his chest, guards the old woman and her candy with a ready beak. I put myself between the steam and the street, the rumor and the riddle, and the girl with the milk poses for me, the parrot does, and, more reluctantly, so does the old candy maker, Argelia, who has sold her latest batch of sweet black eyes to her friend, my mother-in-law.

"Try some," Nora says.

I shake my head, No. No thank you.

"Beth," Bill says. "I thought you were going to try. It *is* good candy."

"Ay," Nora says now. "Ay." Swatting one hand through the air to knock my bad manners away.

Soon enough we are off to San Sebastián, a former guerrilla stronghold, I am told. Look for bullet holes. Swallow your ring. Four times we get lost, and four times—on highways, on rotted roads, in the clogging air between broken adobe towns and metal shantytowns, we are put back on the path by dusty children, old men, women with baskets of mangoes upon their heads. When we seem to know where we are going, we stop the jeep again, and from a boy peddler on the highway we buy three wide boats of *leche de burro*—hardened concoctions of milk and sugarcane, something, my mother-in-law tells me, for the maids. The boy is grateful for the sale, rubs a speck of ash from his eye with a blackened hand. Jeremy waves to him from the back of the jeep, and the boy returns the greeting. Hello. Goodbye. A friend for just one instant.

San Sebastián, when we find it, is bullet pocked. The colors here don't smudge together—they explode and hold their own. The carmine threads left drying in the sun. The lime-colored ribbon in a horse's mane. The yellow pinafore against the pink dress against the basket of bright red petals, no they are not petals, but the twitching crests of live chickens, tied down with a string, ready to sell. There is, it is true, a geography of bullet holes—walls unplugged, roofs open to rain, some holes big as hearts and the radiating fissures, like lines of blood. We walk the streets—Bill, Jeremy, me, Nora—and all along the way there are portraits wanting to be taken, there are reasons not to be afraid. *Foto,* the townspeople call to me. *Foto. Take me. Take me. Por favor.* They arrange themselves about their plates of peeled cucumbers, on their little thrones of dust, they settle the plastic jugs of water on their heads. They arrange themselves beside the coffins they sell from their street-front funeral homes, behind the fabric looms that they work with their bare feet, on their crowded pickup trucks, where they wear thin strips of lace upon their head, as if this will protect them from the heat. They throw themselves about the pillar of a church. It is a suffering beauty, it is two boys with a blue bucket thrown inverted over both their heads, and then their father calling to them, or maybe an uncle, a friend—telling them to pose for me. Arm over arm. Then hand in hand. My knees in the dust, my own neck naked, the diamond on my finger turned toward the palm of my hand, I feel something pass away inside, something like joy blowing in. It is December 31, the final day of the millennium.

That night I stand on the streets of Santa Tecla and watch El Salvador toss its colors to the sky. They have been selling the fireworks all week long from temporary tables in the park, from dug-out caves in market walls, and every possible explosive is on display—the kinds kids stomp on, the kinds that need a match, the kinds that require both a torch and some sort of cannon contraption to hurl the chemicals heavenward. It's the sound and smell of ammunition, a horrendous pop pop pop pop pop, with the occasional bomb thrown in, and up among the stars it's huge twisters of light, storming swirls of red and blue, crackling snaps of electric white. Across the street from Nora's house, the neighbors Mike and Flora are having a party; Mario, Bill's brother, is charming the crowds. Beside Nora, Rafael's mother is hosting a gig. Around the corner, Beto, Bill's uncle, is serving drinks and I huddle with Jeremy wherever we go, overwhelmed by the monstrosity of the party. On a TV somewhere, they're beaming in a talent show from Mexico. In a garden behind the coils of concertina wire, they are serving hot turkey and ham. And now someone's unrolled a block's worth of firecrackers on the street, and they've been lit and they go off hissing, scream-ing, hurling, a full five-minute extravaganza. At midnight pre-cisely Bill is across a garden from Jeremy and me, surrounded by his mother, his aunts, his friends, laughing his fast, ricocheting Spanish laugh, smiling. Someone screams that it's the year 2000, and a drunk man smacks my forehead with a kiss.

*W*e visit the farm the next day, arriving an hour before dusk, arriving when they do: the itinerant coffee pickers looking for work in the hills above El Limón. In the back of Nora's jeep, Ana Gabriela, Nicha and Selena, my husband, my son sit in a cramp on broken seats. It is the height of picking season in El Salvador. Already the cherries on the trees have mostly ripened to red, and in some places the cherries are already gone, siphoned off the trees a few weeks before by facile hands.

"I want to tell you something about Ana Gabriela," Nora is yelling over the noise, yelling in English, for my sake and also for the sake of the little girl, who speaks only Spanish. I sit beside Nora, knocking my head against the jeep's metal roof as it hisses and bounds over the terrain, as Nora, shaking her head, throws the vehicle and the rest of us into a more proficient gear. "Mutt gave birth the other day, and Ana Gabriela found her," Nora hollers the story, both hands on the wheel now, pressing forward. "It was one of the strays, down the hill, a messy business, nobody's dog. But Ana Gabriela sang to every one of those pups. Took them up into her arms and held them, like she was already a mother." Nora hits a hole in the earth and throws all of us forward, then shakes her head, her mind still on Ana Gabriela. "Dirtiest things you've ever seen," Nora repeats herself. "And she sang to each one like she was a mother."

I turn around to catch a glimpse of the girl. She is looking out the window, her curly hair on Jeremy's shoulder. Jeremy, transfixed and deaf as well to Nora's story, takes her shoulder as a brother would and watches the landscape fly by in amazement. He doesn't remember this place, I'm thinking. He was too young the last time we jeeped through the hills.

"Beth," Nora yells now. "Beth. I want to show you something. Look here, Beth. Look there. Delicious, Beth. Delicious."

I nod. I breathe in the dusty, coffee-laden air.

"Beth," Nora yells again.

"Yes?"

"Beth!" She hadn't heard me.

"And now look there, Beth. See? Over there. It's Tiburcio's house, do you see it, Beth?"

"I do."

"And behind Tiburcio's house is the piece of farm I've left to Jeremy. Delicious."

$\mathcal{A}$t night, inside the farmhouse that Don Alberto built and Nora's fitted out as her own, darkness is a blindness, and then a panic, a thin surrender. No light leaks in, and the air lies heavy with insecticide, a suffocating balm. In the bedroom Nora, Bill, Jeremy, and I share, I cannot see and I cannot breathe. Even as I glare at the darkness, even as I suck on my own lungs, it is impossible, and finally I cut loose from the sheets and feel my way out of the claustrophobia, toward the night. My presence there stirs the guards who are paid to keep us safe. It stirs the birds called *urraca,* who sing their mischief, and the frogs, down by the springs. It stirs my husband, who joins me now and insists that I look up, at the jewelry of the stars, which seem closer and within reach at this altitude. "It's like a Christmas tree," Bill says. "Like candles. Look up. You'll see. Every star is the brightness of Venus." Glitter rains down from Orion's belt. Something rustles in the nearby underbrush, and the guards across the way flicker their lights.

I breathe.

I see the light of Venus.

Fifteen years ago not a soul on this planet could have convinced me that I'd be sleeping here, in Don Alberto's house, at night. But now on the veranda we sit, Bill and I, while inside our son sails on the boat of his weary bed, the springs beneath him sloshing and careless, the air above him a weight. There is no need for us to speak. We are each in our own place, and I know from watching him that Bill is remembering youth, grandfather, brothers, friends, the *pupusas* at the end of the day. He is remembering water holes and scorpions; the mules that obeyed the treacherous trails; a flock of parakeets, their song. He is remembering the men who brought the coconuts down from their trees, and Lenora, slapping tortillas on the grill, and all the family history of the hills here, at St. Anthony's Farm. Nora is inside, fast asleep in the bed beside my son. She is sixty-seven years old now, her hair is all white, her one leg is braced, her husband is gone, her sons don't live here anymore, and her little companion, Ana Gabriela, is sleeping in the second room beside the maids. This is Nora's country. This is her land. Now it is Nora who coaxes the trees toward their yield.

Earlier this evening, before this pitch-black night, before the dawn that will turn on the lights, I watched Nora with Nicha, her favorite maid. I watched the two of them sitting in the diminishing evening, digesting their tortillas and beans, Nicha telling stories with her hands, her hips, her stomping bare feet, telling only fractionally with her voice. Nicha's chin jutting out past her lips. Her lips revealing nothing when she smiled. Every story she told was a pantomime. Every story an invitation, so I watched, I understood about Nicha's dozen kids, about the ones who died, about the father they'd had, about his deafness, his sourness, his complaints. I understood how Nicha beat her husband with a whack, a punt, an elbow, a stranglehold whenever he accused her of lying down with other men, whenever he raised his own greedy fingers to other girls. I understood an evening, entirely, in Spanish.

Tell me about when you were a jerk, Nora had been saying, and Nicha, her hands on her hips, her eyebrows arched in mock surprise, had bowed into a past made extravagant by time, into intrigues Nora surely knew but was glad to know again, tales that forced tears from both these white-haired women's eyes. It had gone past dusk. It was a baroness and a maid, their friendship under the cover of night.

"Did I ever tell you about my mother?" Bill whispers now, in the dark, the Christmas show still gallant above us, his mother and our son inside, asleep, Nicha and Ana Gabriela and the others in the maid's quarters, across the way. "Fundación Salvadorena de la Tercera Edad," he says. "Did I ever tell you about that?" Bill's voice is quiet. Peaceful. His American voice. His American accent.

"No." I take his hand into mine because the birds seem close, because I am suspicious of all that the night keeps shadowed, invisible. Because it has always been, *Did I ever tell you about my grandfather* until now, and because perhaps only I am aware of the noun that's been changed in the sentence. "No, I do not know that story," I say. "What are the words supposed to mean?"

"Fundación Salvadorena de la Tercera Edad is a community," Bill says. "Of homeless people. In a renovated house. People too poor, too old, too sick for even the government to care."

"And so your mother . . . ?"

"My mother's the president, has been volunteering there for thirty years. She raises money, crazy schemes. She keeps it on its feet."

I am amazed that after all these years this is a fact I did not know. "Crazy schemes?"

"Bus tours with her friends, aluminum can drives, all kinds of community projects."

"What do you mean bus tours?" I wonder.

"She rents the bus, she hires the driver, she maps out destinations in Honduras, Guatemala, Nicaragua, wrangles every imaginable discount. And then she sells tickets to all of her friends and they go off touring in their ritzy, old-lady way, and when the tour is over, Nora has more cash for the Fundación Salvadorena de la Tercera Edad. It pays the rent. It buys them blankets. It feeds thirty every day."

"You never told me that."

"Well. And every Christmas she goes door to door, asking for turkeys."

"For turkeys?"

"She gets donations, and then she cooks them herself. You know how she does things."

"Yes."

"She's tough, but she's got a good heart."

"Yes, she is. And yes, she does."

"She was always volunteering. Always. I remember her dragging me around from place to place, when I was a kid. I remember the people from the Fundación. They were characters back then. Everyone knew them."

"What do you mean?"

"Well. For example. There was the Cousin."

"The Cousin?"

"He'd pretend he was related to every wealthy Salvadoran family—he'd stop you in the street and tell you everything about a family tree, and where they lived, and where they got their money from, and then, of course, how they were related to him. So we called him the Cousin."

"But he was homeless."

"Yes. And then there was Toño Give Me Five, because he was always asking for five cents. And Paco Diarrhea, named for his frequent stomach ailments, who was the most famous one of all. My mother and her friends would make up errands for him and then give him money for doing what they had never needed done. I don't know what was wrong with Paco; maybe he was autistic. But when he died Nora and the others organized a funeral for him, bought him a casket, got the whole town to come. They made him important."

"I can picture it."

"Back then every one was a character; we knew them.

Today, as with everywhere else, I guess, the homeless people of my hometown are just crazy, or they're poor. They're anonymous."

"Except with your mother."

"Except with her."

"Why are you telling me this? Why right now?"

"Because today when you were playing with Ana Gabriela she told a story."

"About what?"

"About a man who went blind with his own cataracts. A man from the Fundación. Old man. Homeless."

"And what happened?"

"Nora got a doctor to do the operation, and now the guy can see. First time in years. He's walking around and now he sees. He never knew what Nora looked like before. Now when she's there, she says, she always gets his blessing."

*B*y dawn, the pickers are in place, each family assigned a line of trees by Nora's supervisor, Tito, who has donned a new shirt because we've come. We walk the accelerated angles of the dirt roads before we find them—Nora with her leg brace like a flint against the sun, a pointed stick in her hand to poke off dogs, a straw hat smashed down upon her head, the pulp from the stolen orange on her lip. Roosters gang about her ankles, and baby chicks, and often at the edge of the road she stops, and out of nothing materializes a plenitude—the dust first, and then the people, the antiqued women and their children and their children as well, and sometimes there are children after that, never precisely clear just who belongs to whom, though Nora knows, Nora says, *This is Lola, and this is Lucia, and this is Selia's mother-in-law. And that boy there is that husband's sister's, and those kids are not brothers but second cousins.* All in Spanish, but it no longer feels secondhand. All in Spanish I learn who leaves their babies strung up in the hammocks, between trees, who still believes in the value of picking beans.

Nora even knows who steals which oranges from whose trees, and she pretends she doesn't know these things when the campesinos invite her to their shacks. *Come here*, an old woman beckons to us as we walk the slope at dawn. *Sit here,* she says, as we make our way through the opened gate and find the kitchen, which is really just a fire and a blackened pot, no roof overhead. One table. Two chairs. Nora sits down. The ancient woman with the white roped hair extends her family's only orange. *They need to feel that I've been a guest in their house,* Nora says to me in English. *They need to have something to give.*

I have an orange for you, I saved it for you. This is my gift. Please. Allow me to give it. The woman splits the thing right apart with her hands. Nora lets the pulp dry, a testament, on her chin. Two little girls in tattered dresses point and giggle. The ancient, aproned woman waves her hands, exuberant. Chickens are everywhere, their beaks hard as dried corn, and an altar, made of colored foil, steaming in the sun. This is the house of hospitality.

And then we're off the dirt road and into the thicket of trees, branches weaving into branches, a verdant stiffened cloth. Nora goes first, and then my son, then me, then my husband, and then the two guards, who point their rifles up toward the sky. We bend the branches away from our faces, so many dark green gates. In the near distance, we see what we can see—the occasional scatter of knapsacks, plastic bags of exotic purple juice, the crinkle of dead leaves on the ground, an astonishing adobe structure, nearly consumed by fire and time, that Nora cannot remember ever having seen before, on her own farm.

At last we hear what we have come for: the sound of pickers picking, somewhere close, up ahead. It's like warm rain on a roof, or birds dropping seeds, softness knocking against softness. When we find them, we find them just one at a time, everything obscured by the lushness save the one particular tree and its one particular picker at that time. He sifts his cherries into his hat. She wears her basket about her neck like a giant pendant and moves her hands up and down the tree's pregnant limbs, so that it is an animal she tames, an animal: yielding. And then there are the kids.

"Beth," Nora says, from somewhere beyond my immediate vision. "Beth, come here. Follow my voice." I push through gate after gate, the leaves of the trees thwacking gently across my face. "My oldest picker, Beth. Here he is. Eighty-two years old. Delicious, Beth. Delicious." He is shorter than I am, his face practically oriental, his hair hidden by his hat until he swabs away the hat and brushes his soft white fuzz into place with a sticky hand. He straightens his collar. He bows, modestly. He poses for my camera: a solid gaze, a prideful stance. He wants to be here, Nora tells me. He takes pride in the strength he still has.

"See what he does," Nora says. "See how he picks." And I stand beside him, follow the workings of his gnarled hand, move my own fingers among the cherries in imitation. Liberated, the cherries fall, and the old man looks at me and laughs, then stoops to find the rubies among the dead things on the ground.

There is an art to coffee picking. There is history. Squeeze the cherries and get two glistening water drops, and what you hold, so the saying goes, is good. What you hold is ripe.

*L*ater, at one o'clock, a gypsy procession transports the cherries to the top of the hill, to a hardened plate of dust, a small plateau. The cherries arrive in bags and baskets, on shoulders, upon heads. They come up against accelerating angles—up a road without mercy, on labor-hardened backs. Two little boys in blue shirts share one load. One miniature man takes on a rattled, busted sack. A family of four distributes their weights, and a woman near full-term with child will not ask for help. Out from the shacks along the side of the road, the old women and the little kids and the starving dogs and their pups come to honor a day's labor, to honor trees, to honor what the earth gives up, while on the plate of dust the first arrivals sit, sorting the red fruits from the green, this work that only hands can do, and only peasants will.

The vanity here is cherries and their weight. The pride is in the picker's back—impossibly straight beneath impossible loads, against roads that cut up high to heaven like an old machete knife.

This man's face a map of lines.

This woman's dress a costume of threads.

These two brothers in their blue shirts, their faces greased with grime, their smiles like a scandal in the sun.

This convocation of hands. This knowledge.

And now Nora the baroness and Tito the supervisor and Tiburcio with a fistful of ropes take their respective places, and now Ana Gabriela, whom I suddenly discover in the shadows, holds a new chick in her hands, and now there is the serious, slow shuffling assemblage of burlaps and families and sweat. What the fruits have to say to the scale, to the ledger where Nora writes the harvest down—each picker now matched with a number of kilos, each person equated with a sum, Ana Gabriela laughing and Nora catching her laughing as Tito slides the bar across the horizontal of the scale and Nora stands ensconced behind her desk and Tiburcio ties up the bags. Every weight is a grade, a measure, a fact fixed on a page, and one by one Nora calls the picker's name, and bag by bag the cherries are thrown upon the scale and weighed. *Oli,* Nora calls to

Nicha's daughter. *Manuel, Rigo, Mercedes, Concha, come here, bring me your beans.* And these are the fates, these are the offerings, this is a day's work, a yield. An indication of the month to come, on St. Anthony's Farm, El Salvador.

Pinch a cherry between your thumb and finger. If it cries two tears, it is ripe. Give a woman her father's farm. If she loves his land, she'll love his people.

*W*e will stay in El Salvador eight days. Every day will feel like four or five—each one splintered into stretches of suffocating incarcerations behind barricaded walls, then breaking open, over and over, into something unexpected, liberating, and, at the same time, blinding. The funeral of a stranger that walks its way down a dirt road. The garden of lettuce inside the white orphanage walls. The communities grown up on meridian strips between asphalt highways. The cubbies in the supermarket where the patrons check their guns. The place my husband's aunts and friends and mother make for me on the couches, in the gardens, walled in by bricks. In the outdoor marketplace, where I am told to be most cautious, the children follow me through the overbearing aisles, between fruits I've never seen before and babies asleep upon piles of hard green tomatoes, between smoking tortilla grills and unhusked corn. They follow me, giggling, touching my hand, giggling again, then, at the market's edge, break into a run toward old, fallen steps. They want their picture taken. They pose. They laugh outrageously when they hear the click, and then they scramble and pose for me again. *Pupusas,* they call. *Pupusas. Foto. Gracias,* I say. And that is all. It is the snapping of the photographs now that matters, and not the images I'll later hold in my hand.

In between the dangers and adventures, inside the lulls that rise like waves inside Nora's city house, I seek out the little girl, little dark-haired Ana Gabriela. I teach her the games we brought with us—the red monkeys in the blue barrel, the three-dimensional tic-tac-toe—conveying the rules with a little Spanish, with a lot of gestures, with the help of Jeremy, who demonstrates. I will watch her giggle at our overwrought theatrics—her hand over her crooked-toothed mouth—and she will disappear and then return with cookies she has stolen from the maids for our sake, or a pillow from the couch, or the shoes of her Barbie doll. With every game Jeremy and I teach, she insists on giving something in return, scouring Nora's house for whatever she thinks she can give away, until we are all out of gifts, on either side. She lets me hug her, and I do. She laughs with Jeremy. She is at my side more and more, this gentlest shadow, allowing me in with my abortive, flattened Spanish. And when we are coming or going I'll see her teaching the maids how to string the monkeys in a chain, how to slip the colored disks into the portable tic-tac-toe.

She thinks you are very beautiful, Nora tells me, for little Ana Gabriela, whose mother has gone missing, whose feet make no sound on the cool white tile of that house. It is not a word that resides with me, not a word that fits, and again I sink to my knees and take the child in my arms and say, "No, Ana Gabriela, you are." Eight days have passed, and we are leaving soon—I, Bill, Jeremy, who stands with Nora, practicing some Spanish. Soon, I think, I will be gone, safe, where there are no razors on the walls, where my own gold heart will fall down lightly on my chest, where it is a new millennium. I look around. I study things. I wonder. That's when I hear the sound of metal on metal, the sound of a stem between two blades. It's Ana Gabriela—escaped into the garden, and now returned. She has cut me three red roses, fat as suns.

Coffee picking

BEGINNINGS, AGAIN

⸺⸺⸺

*N*early a year after I left behind the three red roses the U.S. Department of Agriculture would not allow me to keep, Nora calls with the news that she has turned Don Alberto's old-brick house at St. Anthony's Farm into her own *zapote*-colored dwelling, a painstaking, loving renovation. A few weeks later she calls again; she has had a party at the house, it is delicious, she is happy.

But increasingly I grow mad with the writing of this book, laid low with the weight of all these words. More and more, I read Jeremy passages, stopping in mid-sentence, *Do you understand? Can you imagine?* He sits slung across the pin-striped love seat while I hover over my messy desk, insisting the past into the present, polishing stones. "This is where you come from," I say. "Only half of where I come from," he answers. The corrective salve of a child's perspective.

By early January, a fever has set in. At first the heat is not in my skin, but in my mind, where memory collides with imagination and where my thoughts turn helplessly to fault lines and fissures, to subduction zones and triple junctions, to the unsettled business of the never-finished earth and the frailties that still quaver beneath a marriage. I have loved the same man the whole of my adult life—have been rescued by his calm, buoyed by his mind, delivered to a kinder place by his art, his hands, his eyes, his kiss in the deep of our long night. And I have trespassed, stolen, insisted, begged, but I have no certain claim upon his past. We are separate people, and there is no cure for that; language cannot finally bridge the gap. I lie in bed during the darkest hours but never sleep. It's early January 2001, and I feel alert to something I cannot conjure, afraid of something I cannot name. I am anxious, a vigilante. I seek. I fail. I wait.

Uneasiness is its own sequester. At last, for reasons I again cannot quite articulate, I type out an email to Adela, asking her, with little prefatory chatter, to remember October 10, 1986. It's news of an old earthquake I'm looking for, I tell her, the big 7.5er that struck San Salvador just a few months after my first visit to the country, leaving the capital and its surrounds a murderous wreck. Hotels and office buildings fell to their knees and buried hundreds. Four of the six city hospitals collapsed. The Metropolitan Cathedral, the National Library, the National Museum, the U.S. Embassy were scarred and crippled; the Tower of Democracy lost all its windows, one killing crash. In the middle of the war, the earth reminded a tiny nation that it was bigger, in the end, than any politics and all of hatred, as hundreds died and tens of thousands were injured and hundreds of thousands lost their homes. Nevertheless, the army concerned itself with the guerrillas. *I've been thinking about that earthquake*, I write to Adela, in the middle of the night. *I've been wishing that I could imagine what it was like.* I press "send," then wish I could clutch the email back, could be less selfish with my need to know and to imagine, less vigilant and on the prowl. I go to bed. I do not sleep. Two mornings later I find Adela's answer; I find, in other words, forgiveness implicit.

Dear Beth, she begins. *Last night I was reading a story in a magazine you wrote, and I'm enjoying it so much, I'm so admiring your talent. I am proud of you, Beth, and when I tell people of you, I always say, "She is my nice."*

The earthquake you ask of was October. I was at the Embassy when it happens, I was getting airline tickets for one of my bosses, when suddenly I heard this explotion. I thought it was the guerrilla putting a bomb at the Embassy, then I turned around and I saw the wall cracking, then everything started shaking, bottles of cristal water were exploding, and everyone started running outside. You could see from the parking lot all the dust from all the fallen buildings in downtown San Salvador, and I left at once to get home to Santa Tecla. When I got home, my son Steven wasn't there, and I started crying as there was no sign of him, and finally he showed up—he had been running from San Salvador to Santa Tecla. That night we slept in the living room, there were lots of tremors, the lights were out, and on top of that it was raining. I put my jewelry and some cloths in a small suitcase, and every time there was a tremor we ran to the garden with my suitcase. What an ordeal, I will never forget that day. I was really frightened. The funny thing is that when I was at the Embassy I thought of my sisters and my brother, I thought, What if something happened to them, and on the other side of the city, in Santa Tecla, they were thinking about me. There is more about the earthquake, but I will never finish, so maybe this very little will be of help.

Lots of kisses to you always.

Love.

By noon, the fever has volleyed and reached my skin. I can't get warm enough despite two sweaters, a vest, a coat, my mittens, then all of the sudden I'm hot as hell. I stay at my desk as long as I can, collect Jeremy from school at two, come home, wrap myself in blankets, and collapse. I feel Jeremy's kisses on my forehead, cool and wet to mark the hours. I don't wake until it's dark. The night is a play in three torrid acts—hot, cold, then hot again; I am soaked and I am shaking. In the morning I am sicker than I've been for many years.

And the day lumbers forward and the fever lingers and I am useless and dull until, at five o'clock in the afternoon, the phone rings for the first time all day. I know at once from the way my husband's voice is changing, that it is Nora, and that there is news, and that it is not good. Many are dead. Many are buried. Santa Tecla lies in smolders.

It is January 13, and the earth, it seems, has parted its jagged jaws and roared. Nora, Bill learns, was in her carport when it happened, returning from a baptism and looking ahead to the afternoon, when she heard the bellow and felt the pavement beneath her move. What had been solid became liquid ooze. What had been level rose like molten concrete waves, so she went up and down but not forward as she ran toward an open space where only sky was at risk of crashing down.

Down the street, meanwhile, and over a hill, in a neighborhood of Santa Tecla called Las Colinas, mansions were tumbling from the sky, plunging from their mountain berths in a storm of dust and drama. Whatever was in their path fell prey—the clustered houses that sat on the mountain's lower face, the children spinning tops in the narrow streets, the idle conversations between neighbors. Before there was time to look up and run, a swath of suburbia was swallowed whole, entombed in a mudslide that stopped six blocks short of Nora's front door. Those who were saved were saved because of luck—because of an errand that had taken them away from home, because of a traffic jam that had delayed their return, because of a plate of hot tortillas they were delivering to a neighbor. Because of a baptism that had ended on time, not minutes later, when the cathedral would be lying in splinters.

An earthquake has struck, 7.6 magnitude this time, centered off the southern coast, big and mean enough to make a name through Mexico, cleaving earth from earth, leaving chasms and capillaries. The world won't know the news for hours. The phone lines have just now opened up; the connection is surreal and tenuous.

"An earthquake," Bill mouths the words to me while he listens to his mother.

I mouth back, "An earthquake? A bad one?"

He shakes his head up and down then left to right, and then he stops and angles himself away from me, lifts his hand up officiously as if to halt the questions I haven't started asking; finally he leaves the room where I am lying and trails off with his Spanish. I think of what he must be thinking, of how far away Pennsylvania must seem from home, how oddly tranquil this house must feel crushed up against his mother's chaos. I think of how he must be remembering himself as an eight-year-old boy, as a child yanking a two-year-old brother from a crib and running both of them to safety over roiling ground, in the middle of the night, in the middle of an earthquake, the last earthquake that he lived through.

An earthquake is a sudden slip caused by stresses in the earth. A fault is all that has been crushed between two blocks of rock. An instant is what it takes for a city to be swallowed. I am guilty of imagining this. I am guilty, with a fever. In the other room, I hear Bill's silence, then his words. I hear him gathering himself around the shock he didn't see coming.

It is impossible to stop the land from speaking, impossible to ordain it with a conscience, impossible to teach it, to persuade it: This is a family, this is a child, this is a people's history; leave it be. It is impossible to win out over earthquakes, and now Bill is altogether silent, and I hear the click of the phone. He comes to me. I turn to him. He remembers. I imagine.

"An earthquake," he says.

"A bad one?" I ask him.

"A bad one," he says. "A really bad one."

Later that night the first images reel in on the news. "Santa Tecla," the correspondent is saying, "this morning, near noon," and the screen fills with mounds of newly erupted dirt, nothing but dirt, and with people digging with their hands, or no longer digging, just walking over the mounds of dirt, calling the names of those who must be buried deep within, who might still be alive, who can't be rescued, calling, calling, their voices hardly human. Like Pompeii leavened with a volcano's ash, Las Colinas has been entombed, lies, the correspondent is estimating, some ten feet below the surface, and Bill starts talking about what Las Colinas was, how Las Colinas hadn't been a neighborhood at all back when Bill was a kid, but a coffee farm, a pretty one, with an in-built labyrinth of catacombs and caves.

"That was a farm," Bill says, more to himself than to me, more to kick his heel in, regain his footing. "And it was a gorgeous place, thick with trees." He stops and shakes his head. He runs his fingers through his whitening hair. "We'd take our horses up there, and we'd go exploring in the caves that had wormed in through the earth over time: Mario, Dad, and me, our friends. We always suspected that the caves had been carved by water, by long dried-up underground springs."

Now those caves are gone, rumbled to nothing, and so are the houses that sat upon them, and so are the people who called those houses home. Buried ten feet deep under the quake-induced mudslide are little girls and little boys, multiple generations of single families, newlyweds and widows, lovers and gardeners and maids, none of them properly eulogized, none of them ready to die. All across El Salvador the land has tucked up and slammed down, engulfing tourists at a waterfall, swiping coffee pickers off slopes, snuffing out secondary roads, snapping the beautiful things into pieces. The historic, heartening structures are gone: the chapel in the orphanage, the Fundación that Nora helps run, storefronts and offices, the church in which my in-laws were married, where my husband gave his first confession. "You walk by St. Carmen now," Nora had told Bill, earlier, on the phone, "and you see its altar, its Sacred Heart statue; you see these from the street because, my God, there are no walls."

Because earlier that morning Nora had indeed gone walking, had gone out, with her limp leg, searching for everyone she loves. She had walked up and down the streets, knocking on doors. *Are you okay? Do you need help?* She had found her sisters and her brother: alive. Found her best friends and my husband's best friends and their families: all, miraculously, alive. Found her gardener, Tiburcio, who was—by fluke—in the town of Santa Tecla and not out among the coffee trees, and she found Nicha, whom she has known for sixty years. Nora herself had been found and embraced, blessed and questioned: *What now? Are you all right? What did you lose?*

And through the tumult of it all, through the powerful tremors that ensued, through paths that he must have made for himself by chopping down grasses and tree limbs with a machete because the roads were newly smothered, inverted, came Tito; he came with news. All the homes on Nora's farm were down, he reported—the adobe huts in which the campesinos live, the kitchen in which Lenora cooked, the old-brick house that Nora had recently renovated and stuccoed and sweetened with a color she'd told us was not quite like a peach, nor like a cherry, renovated with an eye, a heart, on owning her own legacy. Elsewhere, forty coffee pickers had been lost to a single landslide. Entire slopes of coffee trees

had been ripped from their roots; farm roads would be impass-
able for months. But there was, Tito said, a miracle to report on,
too: He had found Nicha's teenage grandson alive, found him
in the only room of Lenora's old house that had been left
standing after the quake, found him sitting there: spared and
deep in shock.

"I am taking out a loan," Nora tells Bill when he gets
through to her by phone a few days and an estimated eight hundred tremors later. "I am taking out a loan because the first thing
that must get done is building all my workers their new homes."
Already she has had corrugated metal siding taken to Fundación
and banged up, haphazardly, to the wooden joists so that the
infirm old won't have to sleep out in the streets; has talked to
the nuns at the orphanage, asking what needs to be done—and
how fast; has begun to organize delivery of food to the
campesinos in the hills who were trapped by the abrupt collapse
of all the roads. Already she is looking beyond all she has lost—
crystal, china, the house she had renovated, her secret, in the
hills—to ask, What can I do here? What must get done? While
I, here in Pennsylvania, sit in fevered silence, close my eyes, and
see the mudslide coming. Hear the earth roar. Again: see the
mudslide coming.

"That land," a friend writes to me a few days later, when my
fever is in full bloom, "isn't fit to live on." And yes, I think, it's
true. El Salvador is an unstable place; the land has a mean mind
of its own. For as long as there are people there, there will be
earthquakes and volcanoes. For as long as there is a building up,
there will be a brutal wrecking down.

Hola Beth. It is Adela, two weeks later, from an embassy
computer. *Oh Beth, this has been the most horrible experience, worst
than in 86. Why? In 86, the earthquake was only in the city. This was
all over the country, and the worst was Santa Tecla, Comasagua, Los*

Amates, Los Chorros. I have taken some pictures to send you. Maybe they will come out all right.

I want to tell you that Saturday, as you know, I always go to the farm, and Richard, my son, practically lives there, but on Friday he decided to go to the Beach and told me he would be back on the farm Saturday morning. Friday night, I was planning to go to the farm, but Noy called me if I wanted to go with her shopping, and I said yes. About 11.15, I picked Noy up and off we went to Siman, the shopping center. We had been there about 10 minutes when I saw the floor moved like a wave, and all the china at Siman started braking, and when the lights went off, I told Noy to get out of there, and we got in our car, and I thought we were in New York, the traffic was so heavy we hardly could moved.

On the way to Santa Tecla, I told Noy, soon we'll be in Santa Tecla, nothing has ever happened there, we'll be safe, but wrong!!!, First thing we saw a wall on the ground, then we turned to go to Nora's house, and we saw more walls on the ground, and then we saw Tere Parker, and she said that the whole of Las Colinas was gone. When I got to my house, the walls were craked, everything on the floor, the china broken, the roof had fallen, a mess. Meanwhile the phones were out, the cells were out, we couldn't get hold of Richard, and we found out that the epicentro was on the beach. Then I started to tell Nora that I had a feeling something had happened at the farm, but everyone said no, and then I was having lunch when the maid came and said there was a man from my farm looking for me. My heart just turned and I went out and there was Rafael, he was pale, and told me everything was on the ground, his house, my house, everything, the roads were blocked, that I could not go over there. I waited three days until they opened the roads to my farm, and I went up there and brought food to my people. Every day I bring food, cloth, blankets, water, and Don Rodolfo, 82 years old, Rafael, and Don Ines, they insist on staying to watch over the farm. I imagine the fault went through my house, you can see the cracks, which are very deep, then it went on to the church, which by the way is completely on the ground. Now I'm just hopping we can borrow money from the bank to build the worker's houses. I wish I could have the money, I told them to build little houses with tin sheets or whatever they can find there, until I can get some money, for something decent.

To go to Nora's farm its impossible. Roads are blocked, and as it is not a main road it will take some time to opened. She took some food on Saturday, but she can only go up to Tiburcio's, no farther than that. Everyone around her farm went to Tiburcio's and she distributed the food, and they told her that her new home is down, it is destroyed. I think that with Our Lord's Blessing we'll find a way to build something for these people.

Dear Beth, thanks for writing and for worrying, I'll keep you inform of what is happening here, right now we are fine. At night when Richard leaves or the maid goes home, then I go to Nora's and spend the night there. Elba is staying with Nora too, as her house was destroyed. May God protect us. Pray for my country Beth.

Love to all.

*T*pray, of course I pray, but the earth doesn't want to give it up. The earth continues to moan and shiver, to knock its walls of rock against its walls of rock; to speak, to raise its hard mounds of regret. There will be 3,200 powerful aftershocks in the month to come. There will be bulldozers in the streets of Santa Tecla knocking down large swaths of town and market, history. Shopkeepers will be swept out, clean. Scenes once spied from the balcony of Don Alberto's city house will be crumbled out of view. "You will cry when you see this," Nora leaves a message on the phone. "You will cry. Everything you remember is gone."

And then on Tuesday, February 13, one month to the day of the devastating 7.6 monster, a 6.6 tremblor strikes several provinces east of El Salvador's capital, killing more than 170, injuring at least 1,500, flattening San Cayetano, Guadalupe, Verapaz, and Texistepeque, not to mention half the town of San Vicente, where Nora's friend the candy maker lives, where I walked, snapping photographs of innocents, exactly one year earlier. There are patients on the floors of the hospitals, for lack of beds. There are cars piled high on the splintered Pan-American Highway. There are families pitching tents where their houses used to be, or fleeing to parks and sports stadiums, so many sudden refugees. Francisco Flores, El Salvador's president, has lost his office too; he issues pleas for calm and civility from his temporary quarters at a fairground.

But four days later, it happens again. Unbelievably, it happens again—another quake, this one registering 5.3, that sends the panicked thousands out into the streets, away from cracking buildings, away from landslides. Nora can see the clouds of dust rising from the city of San Salvador. She can see the things quivering in her house. She calls her son. I answer the phone, unaware, of course, of what's just happened. "How are you, Nora?" I want to know.

"Well, Beth," she says, and there is silence. "Well, I'm not good, Beth. Not good at all."

"I am so sorry," I say. "I'm really . . ."

"Where is my son?" she interrupts me. "I want to speak to Bill."

"Here," I say. "Here." I hurry a goodbye and hand Bill the phone. I listen to him speak to his mother, the disbelieving gasp as he receives the morning's news about the 5.3 quake that struck, this time, close to the capital. Bill is telling his mother to come here for a while, to get away. He is telling her that he is worried, what can he do? And then all of the sudden he is yelling at her, yelling—the loud voice he rarely uses. He's yelling at his mother, and then he punches the hang-up button on the phone.

"What was that?" I ask, my voice accusing.

"An aftershock," he says.

"Right then?"

"Yes."

"When you were talking on the phone?"

"Yes. Right then. When we were talking."

"What happened?"

"I told her to get off the phone and get out of the house."

"What was she saying?"

"That the whole place was shaking again, that she could feel the ground starting to move."

"My God, Bill."

"I can't believe this."

"I can't believe it either, Bill, and I'm so sorry."

"She doesn't know when it will end," Bill says, his dark eyes full and tremulous. "She's worried that it won't." He shakes his head, runs his fingers through his hair. I step close and kiss him. I kiss him, this man I love.

"But doesn't it have to end, Bill?"

"Nobody knows."

"But what are the experts saying?"

"That nobody knows."

"What does she want to do?"

"I don't know. It's her country, it's my country, breaking apart."

I kiss him again. There is nothing to say. All we can do is hug one another. Come together, hard, and cleave.

*N*ora's photos of the farm arrived just yesterday. It is St. Anthony's the way I never knew it, the way I never imagined it could be. The roads piled deep with the collapsed debris of their own earthen walls. The coffee sorting station reduced to rubble.

The coffee pickers I once picked beside, the babies I once admired, the children I chased through jungle green stand in Nora's photos before their disappeared domains—their little piles of sticks and stones and sheared-off tin. An overturned card table here. A torn blue apron over there. Maybe, if you search hard enough, a shoe. They stand there wearing everything they now own—three thin cotton dresses and a pair of floral slacks— or they sit there in a chair they resurrected, out in the sun, beneath the lovely sky that has become their ceiling, their blue and sacred dome. At the edges of the photographs bursts the wild bougainvillea, its godly redness like an errant plume, and there is a stillness to the photographs, the sound the earth makes after it roars.

And there among it all, above it all, lies the house that Don Alberto made and that Nora made again—the house on the farm in the hills that looks out over coffee that once was cattle, that once was Pipil and before that Maya, that once was absolutely nothing. Like a child's Lego structure kicked apart by an angry foot, the walls and roof and floor lie in random chunks, some of them provocatively plumb, some in horizontal ruins, some arranged throughout the gaping spaces like rudimentary letters. The random order of destruction. The decades of prideful care and growing shoved ruthlessly aside in an instant.

Hope is not here, I think. This place cannot be salvaged. Words cannot possibly bear this weight, take what has happened here and give it purpose. And yet, the more I study these photographs, these faces beside the homes that have been rumbled down to nothing, the better I understand why Nora cannot, will not leave this place, why her son has never really left it, either, why it has become, intractably, a sweet, dark part of me, why the legacy must and will live on, in words and pictures, blood and earth. Because in the sun these people do stand, and at their

tables they do sit, and in the background of so many photographs, they are working to make things right, they are clearing
a space in which they will inevitably begin again, side by side,
with Nora. One man leans over a compass, a surveyor's pad. One
woman balances her baby in her arms. Three men gather before
a single, still-mighty wall. Nora brings them water, beans, tortillas, prayers from the city and from elsewhere. It is anxious
earth they live on, but it is the only earth they have, and it is in
their blood, as it is in Nora's blood, as it is in my husband's
blood, and as it is therefore a river flowing through the heart of
my only son. This is El Salvador, this is a farm, and things will
grow again. Flick the pit of a mango to the ground. Tomorrow
there will be a tree.

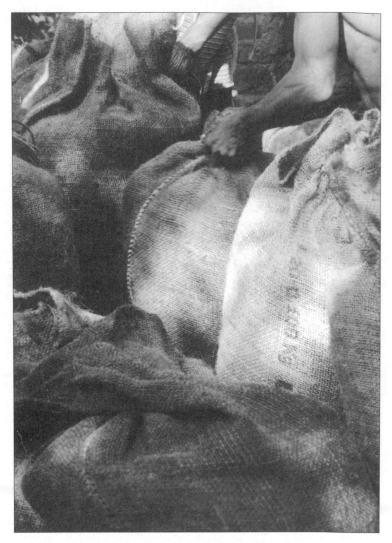

Harvest

APPRECIATIONS

—⟨∞⟩—

Still Love in Strange Places is the product of fifteen years of searching, reading, listening, wanting, and, mostly, asking; it is, therefore, a work that owes a debt to all those who stopped to remember with and for me. For trailing back into the past for my sake, for telling the stories with verve, I am indebted to Bill's glamorous aunt and my friend, Adela Bondanza. For answering the prayers of a country devastated by rapacious quakes and tremors, I am indebted to Sandra Gilmour, Bart and Barb Whitman, Earline Eck, John McClintock, Joan Anderson, Victor Wilson, and all the good souls of my own St. John's Presbyterian Church, as well as my exquisitely generous and consistently caring parents, Lore and Kep Kephart. For giving fragments of this story space in their magazines, I thank the editors of *Salon.com* and *Madison*. For sharing the hard rock of her intelligence and the kind reserves of her soul, I thank my friend Alyson Hagy. For listening while I dreamed out loud, I thank my friend and agent, Amy Rennert. For doing so well all those things that matter so much, I thank W. W. Norton's Stefanie Diaz. For going beyond the call of duty with this text, I thank my manuscript editor, Otto Sonntag. For caring urgently and brilliantly about books that matter, for believing that I could get it right, for opening the door, I thank my friend and editor, Alane Salierno Mason. For lighting the way into every day, for filling this house with grace and joy, for wanting to know how the story will turn out, I thank my sensational son, Jeremy. And for sharing all that he is with all that I've become, I thank my gentle Salvadoran husband and my very dearest friend, Bill.

ACKNOWLEDGMENTS

—⟨∞⟩—

All writers stand on the shoulders of those who have gone before. In this case, *Still Love in Strange Places* would have been impossible without the benefit of those authors who wrote so well about Salvadoran geomorphology, ecology, agriculture, history, culture, and politics. Those who shone the brightest lights include Thomas P. Anderson, *Matanza, The "Slaughter" That Traumatized a Nation* . . . , 2d ed. (1992); Manlio Argueta, *One Day of Life* (1980); Robert Armstrong and Janet Shenk, *El Salvador: The Face of Revolution* (1982); Asociación Cafetalera de El Salvador, *The Story of El Salvador Coffee* (1939) and *Coffee Facts and Fantasies* (n.d.); Barbara L. Beck, *The Ancient Maya*, rev. ed. (1983); Raymond Bonner, *Weakness and Deceit: U.S. Policy and El Salvador* (1984); Jeff Brauer et al., *On Your Own in El Salvador* (1995); Charles D. Brockett, *Land, Power, and Poverty: Agrarian Transformation and Political Conflict in Central America* (1988); David G. Browning, *El Salvador: Landscape and Society* (1971); William Henry Burt and Ruben A. Stirton, *The Mammals of El Salvador* (1961); Timothy J. Castle and Joan Nielsen, *The Great Coffee Book* (1999); Anthony G. Coates, ed, *Central America: A Natural and Cultural History* (1997); Michael D. Coe, *The Maya*, 6th ed. (1999); Gregory Dicum and Nina Luttinger, *The Coffee Book: Anatomy of an Industry from Crop to the Last Drop* (1999); Joan Didion, *Salvador* (1984); Lois Donaldson, *El Salvador in Story and Pictures* (1943); Richard Haggerty, *El Salvador: A Country Study*, 2d ed. (1990); Adam Kufeld et al., *El Salvador* (1990); Aldo A. Lauria-Santiago, *An Agrarian Republic: Commercial Agriculture and the Politics of Peasant Communities in El Salvador, 1823–1914* (1999); Don Moser, *Central American Jungles* (1975); Liisa North, *Bitter Grounds: Roots of Revolt in El Salvador* (1981); Natascha Norton and Mark Whatmore, *Central America* (1993); New America Press, *A Dream Compels Us: Voices of Salvadoran Women* (1989); Lilly de Jongh Osborne, *Four Keys to El Salvador* (1956); Jeffery M. Paige, *Coffee and Power: Revolution and the Rise of Democracy in Central America* (1997); Mark Pendergrast, *Uncommon Grounds: The History of Coffee and How It Transformed Our World* (1999); David R. Reynolds, *Rapid Development in Small Economies: The Example of El Salvador* (1967); Philip L. Russell, *El Salvador in Crisis* (1984); Larry Towell, *El Salvador* (1997); David Rains Wallace, *The Monkey's Bridge: Mysteries of Evolution in Central America* (1997); Alastair T. White, *El Salvador* (1973).